Uncle John's
BATHROOM
PUZZLER

365
NEW
LOGIC
PUZZLES

PORTABLE
PRESS

Bathroom Readers' Institute
Ashland, Oregon, and San Diego, California

Uncle John's Bathroom Puzzler
365 New Logic Puzzles

For information, write...
The Bathroom Readers' Institute
P.O. Box 1117, Ashland, OR 97520
www.bathroomreader.com
E-mail: mail@bathroomreader.com

ISBN-13: 978-1-60710-182-6

Printed in the United States of America
First printing: August 2010

1 2 3 4 5   14 13 12 11 10

Thank You!

The Bathroom Readers' Institute sincerely thanks
the following people whose advice, assistance,
and hard work made this book possible.

Gordon Javna

JoAnn Padgett

Melinda Allman

Stephanie Spadaccini

Cliff Post

Megan Boone

Jeff Altemus

Lorraine Bodger

Rob Davis

Jay Newman

Myles Callum

Amy Miller

Monica Maestas

Amy Ly

Sydney Stanley

Brian Boone

Thom Little

Ginger Winters

Jennifer Frederick

Annie Lam

Sophie and JJ

Porter the Wonder Dog

PUZZLE POWER!

Here at the Bathroom Readers' Institute, we spend a lot of time pondering life's important mysteries: What *really* happened to Amelia Earhart? How many toes does a Sasquatch have? If three family members went on separate vacations—and one went to Paris and another took a train—where did each person go, and how did he or she get there? (More clues on page 88.)

A LITTLE LOGIC GOES A LONG WAY

So when Uncle John asked us to put together another book of logic questions, we started researching right away...and called in our resident puzzle expert Stephanie the Splendiferous to help us out. We looked for puzzles that required reason to solve and decided to include a total of 365—so that you, fearless reader, could do one a day and keep your brain brawny. Here's what we came up with:

• **Traditional logic puzzles:** These offer a set of clues and ask you to sort through what's true and what isn't to match up people, places, events, and so on.

• **Word ladders:** Author Lewis Carroll invented the word game we now call "word ladders," in which the object is to change one word into another by changing one letter at a time, using the fewest steps possible. For example, MORE becomes LESS in four steps: MORE, LORE, LOSE, LOSS, LESS. (No proper nouns allowed, by the way.)

• **Mysteries:** We called on the BRI's favorite private eye, Inspector Commodius Loo, to investigate some crimes. See if you come up with the same answers that he does.

• **Wild & Woolly Wordies:** These are visual word puzzles, like this one for "cross-stitch":

```
          S
          T
S  T  I  T  C  H
          T
          C
          H
```

• **Echoes:** These puzzles include homophones—words that sound alike but are spelled differently and mean different things, like "two" and "too."

• **Cryptograms**, anagrams, hidden messages...and even a few surprises.

So now, with your tinfoil thinking cap pulled on tight and your logic skills at the ready, we wish you good luck and happy puzzling.

—Uncle John and the BRI Staff

1. SCHOOL RULES

This morning, the Bathroom Reader school district reversed its decision that allowed the school superintendent to overturn the school board's ruling that found the local principal had no right to fire a teacher who refused to kick out of class a student who did not bring sharpened pencils to school. So if the kid now goes to class with sharpened pencils, will he be allowed to stay?

2. THE PROVERB CODE

In the two common English proverbs below, we've changed all the letters except "S" and "Y": consonants are represented by the letter "B" and vowels by the letter "E." The punctuation is the same. Can you sort out what the proverbs are?

1. E BEEB EBB BES BEBEY EBE SEEB BEBBBEB.

2. E BEBBEBE ES BEBBB E BBEESEBB BEBBS.

3. WILD & WOOLLY WORDY

Can you figure out what word or phrase this stands for?

B K

4. ANAGRAMMIT

An anagram is a word or phrase that's formed by rearranging the letters of another word or phrase. For example, the words "OCHRE SLOP" can be rearranged to get "PRESCHOOL."

What common 10-letter words can you make by combining these shorter words and anagramming them?

1. IRE IVY NUTS

2. EQUINE ROTS

3. MESH PIT NUN

5. TRIANGULAR REASONING

As it is now, if you add up the four numbers on each side of the large triangle below, you'll get three different sums: 18, 16, and 22. But what you want is for each side to equal the same amount. You can accomplish that by swapping two pairs of numbers. What are the swaps, and what number do all the sides add up to?

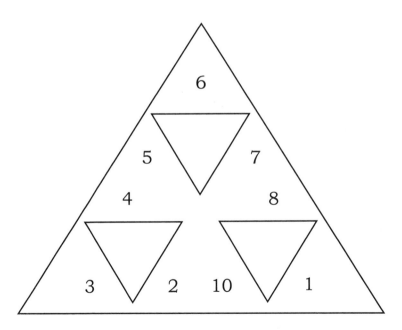

A klazomaniac is someone who always wants to shout.

6. FRATERNAL TRIPLETS

Fill in the blanks with three words that differ by only one letter. The letter will be in the same position in all three words. Here's an example: The students had to _____ carefully to see when the new _____ of chicks would _____. Add "watch," "batch," and "hatch."

"My ____ for tonight," announced the ecologist in an upbeat tone, "is ____ waste." But describing the long-term problems discouraged him so much that after the lecture, he ran straight to a bar for a stiff gin and ____.

7. THREE MEN, THREE JOBS

Adam, Joe, and Alex are—not necessarily in this order—a butcher, a baker, and a candlestick maker. The candlestick maker, who makes the most money, is also a bachelor. Adam makes more money than the baker. He's also Alex's father-in-law, and his wife likes fresh cookies.

Who holds what job?

IOU actually stands for "I owe unto."

8. LANGUAGE EQUATION

If "16 = O. in a P." stands for "16 ounces in a pound," what does this equation stand for?

5 = F. on a H.

The Dead Sea is a lake.

9. THE SWEET SPOT

The owners of the Sweet Spot—a candy store in the mall—love wordplay, and they have a special system for deciding how much to charge for candies. Using the examples below, figure out what they would charge for Sour Drops.

THE SWEET SPOT

LOLLIPOPS $9

JAWBREAKERS $11

CARAMELS $8

CHOCOLATE $9

CANDY CANES $10

SOUR DROPS ....?

Alfred Hitchcock didn't like to make historical dramas because he couldn't...

10. THINK ABOUT IT

What's special about the word SWIMS?

11. ECHOES

What two homophones (words that sound alike but are spelled differently) are being described here?

Cry cotillion

12. DIRECTIONS

Changing one letter at a time, can you go from WEST to EAST in three steps?

13. INSPECTOR LOO AND THE CASE OF THE MISSING BEER STEIN

Inspector Commodius Loo arrived home after a long day on the job and just wanted to relax with a pint of Guinness. But as soon as he walked into his kitchen, he knew all was not right. There on the Formica counter sat four locked wooden boxes labeled (from left to right) oak, elm, cherry, and maple; four numbered keys; and a note:

> Dearest Loo, you swaggering devil—
>
> You've always loved the job and the Guinness more than you loved me, and it's time that I take a stand. Your favorite beer stein is locked in one of these boxes, but it'll take you some time to figure out which one. I'll wait downstairs for five minutes...make your choice. If the beer stein truly means more to you than I do, here are some clues to find it:
>
> **1.** The #4 key opens the cherry or maple box.
> **2.** The beer stein is to the left of the maple box.
> **3.** The beer stein is to the right of the oak box.
> **4.** The #2 key works a lock to the left of the box that holds the beer stein.
> **5.** The #3 key works a lock to the right of the one that takes the #2 key and a lock to the left of the one that takes the #4 key.
> **6.** The #1 key opens the oak box.
>
> Yours truly, Dollface

What box was the good inspector's favorite beer stein in, which key opened it, and what did he do about his sweetie?

14. SAM LOYD CLASSIC: THE PLAYERS WHO ALL WON

See if you can solve this classic by puzzle-maker extraordinaire Sam Loyd (1841–1911):

> Four jolly men sat down to play.
> And played all night till break of day;
> They played for gold and not for fun,
> With separate scores for every one,
> Yet, when they came to square accounts,
> They all had made quite fair amounts!
> Can you the paradox explain?
> If no one lost, how could all gain?

A moment is a real unit of time—it lasts 90 seconds.

15. A DAY AT THE RACES

A husband and wife attending the Big Bad Bug Derby made their predictions: The husband said, "If the snail comes in after the June bug, the butterfly will finish before the centipede." His wife scoffed, "Oh, please. If the butterfly comes in before the snail, the June bug will definitely finish after the centipede."

Turns out they were both wrong. In what order (from first to last) did the bugs finish?

16. QUOTE ME

Rearrange the anagram in the brackets to figure out what President Lincoln was trying to say.

"All I am, or can be, I owe to my [ORGAN HELMET]." —**Abraham Lincoln**

Rachel Jackson was the only American First Lady who smoked a pipe.

17. NESTED WORDS

Like a set of nested eggs, this puzzle requires working from the outside in. First, find a synonym for the second phrase. Then, inside that new word, find a synonym for the first phrase. For example, if the puzzle were "a color in what a lender gives (3, 6)," the answer would be "'RED' in 'CREDIT.'" Now try this one:

A small amount in a great desire (3, 8)

18. SUM FUN!

Starting at the 5, add adjacent numbers by moving horizontally or vertically (but not diagonally) so that they total 32. You can use a number only once—no doubling back!

5	7	2
3	8	6
9	1	4

Life span of a queen bee: three years. Life span of a queen termite: 25 years.

19. CROSS CONFUSION

Can you figure out the purpose of this puzzle and then solve it?

CRY
DUMB
OPEN
CONFRONT
LONG–WINDED

20. RAISING A BET

Gridley, a sportfishing nut, and his buddy Hadley were relaxing and shooting the breeze on the deck of a yacht. Gridley pointed to a 15-foot ladder hanging over the side and said, "I bet you three white sea bass that you can't figure out how much time it'll take for the first three rungs to be covered if the tide rises six inches an hour and the rungs are a foot apart."

Hadley whipped out a pencil and paper, did some figuring, and exclaimed, "Six hours!"

Who had to pay up?

21. IDIOMATIC IDIOSYNCRASIES

In this puzzle, the set of letters below represents the words of a popular English idiom. If CBARAAHP stands for "Caught between a rock and a hard place," what other well-known idiom do the following letters stand for? And what is the missing letter?

RP_PP

22. BEAUTY'S IN THE EYE OF THE BE-OLDER

Denise was a punk-princess pageant winner in her youth, and at her most recent birthday party, she wasn't keen on admitting her age. So she told the guests that if they multiplied her age in 5 years by 5, then multiplied her age in 6 years by 6, and then added the two totals together, they would get a number that is 12 times her current age.

After all that, most of the guests just didn't care how old she was. (Score one for Denise.) But some people did the math—and later, when they wheeled out a large birthday cake ablaze with candles, she knew they had figured her out.

How old is Denise?

14

23. CHAIN REACTION

Insert a word between the two given words to create two new words. For example, adding GUN between BLOW and POWDER would produce BLOWGUN and GUNPOWDER.

GREEN _____ BONE

SAND _____ TENDER

24. WHAT'S COOKING?

You want to cook dinner for the party you're having tonight, but your new house has a bizarre kitchen setup: the range has only three burners that are controlled by three switches in the garage. (We don't know why you picked this house, either.) You need to decipher which switch goes with which burner. You can go out to the garage and turn on the switches as many times as you want, but you can only come inside to check the burners once. How would you figure it out?

25. IT'S SYMBOLIC

The symbols in this puzzle correspond to only three different numbers, but we had some trouble deciphering some of them. Can you figure out what symbol goes with what number, and what the missing numbers are?

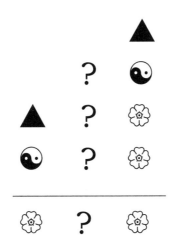

In Japanese, *Nintendo* means "leave luck to heaven."

26. WORDPLAY

Delete one letter from the word below so that the remaining letters (without rearranging them) spell a new word:

SNOWING

Then, delete one letter from the new word so that the remaining letters spell a second new word...and so on, until you run out of letters.

27. HERE FISHY, FISHY

While cleaning out his tank, Jennifer dropped her goldfish Mista down a narrow pipe in her backyard. The pipe was one foot deep, embedded in concrete, and sealed at one end. Mista would certainly have died before Jennifer was able to find something in the house to use to pull him out. All she had on hand were the hose and lemon juice she was using to wash out the tank, and a handful of colorful rocks.

How did Jennifer save Mista before he went to the great fish tank in the sky?

28. MIRROR, MIRROR

A palindrome is a word or phrase that's spelled the same way backward and forward. The three palindromes below are missing some letters. What are they, and what are the right words?

_ A Y _ _

M _ _ _ M

_ E N E _

To fall over, a bowling pin must tilt 10 degrees.

29. LINEAR LOGIC

Move one line in this group of letters to create a common word.

E II I P

30. ANAGRAMMED OPPOSITES

Unscramble these three words to come up with two words that are opposites of each other.

COSY DULY NUN

31. BACKWORDS

Read from right to left—there are two common five-letter words hidden backward in the line of letters below. Do you see them?

T I R E P P U P I L E M A B T A O L F Q

The Chilean rose tarantula can go for two years without eating.

32. A LITTLE NUMBERS LOGIC

Uncle John was thinking of two consecutive numbers between 1 and 10. He wrote them down on two pieces of paper and handed one to Porter the Wonder Dog (who's a *very* smart dog) and the other to Amy.

Porter glanced at his paper and saw the number 9. He told Amy that he didn't know her number. She responded by saying she didn't know his, either. But then Porter declared, "Now I know it!"

What number did Amy have, and how did Porter figure it out?

33. SPELLING STATES

All but three of the 50 United States contain at least one of two particular letters: One is a consonant, the other a vowel. (Some use both.) What are the letters, and what states don't use them?

34. THE SECRET WORD

In this puzzle, the goal is to use the given clues to identify the five-letter secret word. The numbers after each clue tell you how many letters in that word also appear in the secret word. Once you've got the correct five letters, you'll need to arrange them to come up with the correct secret word. See how you do.

— — — — —

SKATE—3
SOAPY—3
PAINT—2
CHORD—1
COURT—0

35. WILD & WOOLLY WORDY

Can you figure out what word or phrase this stands for?

ₚₐᵢNS

36. BACKTRACKING

By reading backward, you can find at least four four-letter words in the given words. You can't change the order of the letters, but you are allowed to skip over letters. Here's an example: in the word TENDER, you'll find RENT, but not REND. How many can you identify?

1. FLESHIER

2. ENTRAILS

37. HAZY DAYS

The day before the day after tomorrow is Sunday. So if Kristen had to take her cat to the vet the day before the day before the day after tomorrow, when was that?

38. DOG SHOWDOWN

Welcome to the Kings County Dog Show, where people and their dogs compete for a blue ribbon and the title of "County's Most Beautiful Human/Canine Pair." At this year's show, there are a total of 22 heads and 72 feet.

How many people and how many dogs are at the show?

39. INSPECTOR LOO MEETS A TUCKERED-OUT EXPLORER

At a pub recently, Inspector Commodius Loo was nursing a pint of Guinness when he overheard the following conversation:

"It was a nightmare, I tell ya," began the grizzled explorer with dust on his boots and sweat on his brow. "I was climbing Mount Everest—a journey that would take six days—but there were only four Sherpas at base camp. And they could only carry four days of food each! I knew I could only carry four days of food myself, so at first I thought the expedition was sunk. But after smoking a good cigar, I figured out how to do it. I made it, but was tuckered out by the time I got to the top."

Loo smirked and looked up from his table. What had taken the explorer an entire cigar to figure out, Loo had managed to deduce in just the time it took to swallow his beer. What had Loo come up with as a solution to the explorer's problem?

40. FRATERNAL TRIPLETS

To complete this puzzle, fill in the blanks with three words that differ by only one letter. The letter will be in the same position in all three words. Here's an example: The students had to _____ carefully to see when the new _____ of chicks would _____. Add "watch," "batch," and "hatch."

"That darned mare ____ us all," the old rancher chuckled, "when she ____ our plans and ____ way out there in the pasture all by herself."

41. MISSING NUMBERS

In the problem below, replace each question mark with either 1, 3, 6, or 7 to make the numbers add up correctly. Each number is used only once.

	2	?	?	8
+	?	4	5	6
	?	1	7	4

42. WORD FIND

What English word meets these criteria? It's six letters long, contains two Fs, two As, one R, and one other vowel.

43. TREED

Some people are just naturally good at clambering around the old family tree and figuring out the complex relationships among individuals. (Others are content with sitting around the trunk drinking lemonade.)

Which group are you in? Can you figure out what relation to you these family members would be?

    1. Your mother's mother's son's son

    2. Your brother's father's stepson's mother

    3. Your sister's daughter's brother's father

44. SCHOOL DAZE

There are 100 kids in Mrs. Gooch's second-grade class. (It's a big class—the result of friendly neighborhood budget cuts.) Of these, 85 children are dropped off at school each day by their parents, 70 carry stuffed animals, 75 like to eat cheese sandwiches at lunchtime, and 80 hate apple juice. What's the least possible number of kids who could embody all four characteristics (meaning, they are dropped off by their parents, carry stuffed animals, like cheese sandwiches, and hate apple juice)?

45. EVERYTHING'S COMING UP RICHES

Uncle Rich is loaded and making out his will. He has three nieces: Jennifer, Daisy, and Diane. Each niece has at least one child. The six grandnieces and grandnephews are Adam, Tom, George, Joe, Emily, and Alicia. Uncle Rich wants each of his nieces' children to get an equal share of his fortune, but his memory is going...so he's not sure how many children each niece has. However, he does remember these six things:

1. Jennifer doesn't have a daughter.

2. Alicia has two brothers.

3. Daisy has the biggest family.

4. Emily doesn't have a brother or a sister.

5. George's brother is six months younger than Tom.

6. Joe is a middle child, but he's the youngest of the boys.

How many children does each niece have, and what are their names?

46. WORD PYRAMID

The pyramid below is supposed to include 10 letters. Your mission is to put the missing seven letters (C, E, G, H, I, K, P) in their proper places so that, connected vertically, they will spell six four-letter words reading down.

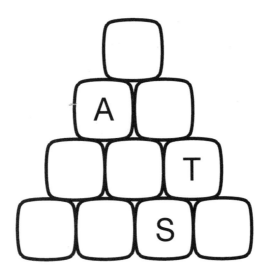

47. ECHOES

What two homophones (words that sound alike but are spelled differently) are being described here?

Help the helper

48. LANGUAGE EQUATION

If "16 = O. in a P." stands for "16 ounces in a pound," what does this equation stand for?

12 = D. of C.

Bill Clinton is allergic to flowers.

49. THIS OR THAT?

What word fits both definitions?

- A tight cluster of people or things
- A hard, round piece of wood

50. BUGGY

Changing one letter at a time, can you go from MOTH to FIRE in four steps?

51. QUICK TRICK

Why would a cobbler in New York rather sell shoes to two Americans than to one Frenchman?

52. NOTABLE QUOTABLE

Below, we've taken a famous quote and turned it into coded text. See if you can puzzle out the real thing.

"QXDVGPEWXTH PGT QJI IWT RADIWTH PCS

QJIIDCH DU IWT BPC. IWT QXDVGPEWN DU

IWT BPC WXBHTAU RPCCDI QT LGXIITC."

—Mark Twain

Those wavy sound lines in comic strips are called "agitrons."

53. FOREIGN EXCHANGE

Last Friday, Saturday, and Sunday, the College of Fun and Design welcomed the first five foreign exchange students of the semester. The young women (first names: Jane, Lisa, Sophie, Samantha, and Rachel; last names: Smith, Jones, Garcia, Pierre, and Chavez) hailed from five home countries: Spain, Poland, Mexico, Canada, and France. Here's what we know about them:

1. Chavez, who's from Europe, got to the school the day before Garcia, who's from North America.

2. The student from Poland came in the day after Lisa and Garcia.

3. No more than two students arrived at the school on a given day. When two arrived, they were from different continents.

4. The students from France and Canada arrived on the same day.

5. Jane and Jones arrived on the same day. Smith came in the day before them.

6. Garcia's first name isn't Jane.

7. Sophie was the only person to arrive on Friday.

8. Rachel arrived on the same day as the student from Mexico.

What are the first and last names of each student, what country is she from, and on which day did she arrive?

54. DYNAMIC TRIOS

We've removed all the consonants from the pairs of words below, but the pairs have something in common. Can you figure out what the common thread is, and what consonants are missing? To help you out, we put the list in alphabetical order.

1. _ O O _ I E _   &   _ I _ _

2. _ A _   &   _ _ E E _ E

3. _ E A _ U _   _ U _ _ E _   &   _ E _ _ _

55. ROAD TRIP

The Nelson and Fisher families left on the same day, at the same time, and from the same place for their summer road trips. However, they headed in different directions. The Nelsons went north, west, south, and east. The Fishers went east, south, west, and north. Each leg of the trip (north, west, etc.) was 1,000 miles long. At the end of the trips, the two families met up in the same place, but they were a few miles away from their starting point. Why?

Q. Who's Rodolfo Alfonzo Pierre Philibert Guglielmi d'Antonguolla? A. Rudolph Valentino.

56. WORD MYSTERY

Use the clues to figure out the mysterious word.

1. I am nine letters long.

2. My 1, 2, and 3 will keep you moving.

3. Without 3, 4, 5, 8, and 9, you might feel a little negative.

4. My 4, 5, and 6 can help you communicate.

5. Put all my letters together, and I'm a craftsman.

What am I?

57. WILD & WOOLLY WORDY

Can you figure out what word or phrase this stands for?

Ancient Greek dentists used stingray venom as an anesthetic.

58. MIX-UP AT THE VET

Four women brought their dogs—Badger, Boomer, Buck, and King—into the Happy Hound Pet Clinic for grooming. In an unusual turn of events, the dogs were all the same breed and color and looked exactly alike. Even more unbelievable: the dogs had the same names as the last names of the four customers, but no woman owned a dog that had her own last name.

The dogs all had their names on collar tags, but the assistant groomer, Cynthia, removed the tags before washing the dogs. That confused things, and Cynthia was having some trouble sorting it all out. Here's what she knows:

1. None of the owners' names have the same number of syllables as their dogs' names.

2. Mrs. King owns Badger, but Mrs. Badger doesn't own King.

Can you help Cynthia deliver the right dog to the right owner so the Happy Hound Pet Clinic doesn't wind up in the doghouse?

59. MIXED MESSAGE

The six letters below can be rearranged into several words. Each letter is used only once, and you have to use all the letters in each word. How many can you find?

E   I   P   R   S   T

60. ECHOES

What two homophones (words that sound alike but are spelled differently) are being described here?

A pan for sautéing a monk

61. BACKWORDS

Read from right to left—there are two common five-letter words hidden backward in the line of letters below. Do you see them?

R A J A H S A R B E M U B L A R O N T A

62. SEQUENTIAL THINKING

What two letters come next in this series?

D R M F S L ? ?

63. MYSTERY NUMBER

What number are these clues are describing?

1. Add its digits together and you get a prime number (a number that's divisible only by 1 and itself).

2. Subtract its first digit from the second and you get 5.

3. The number is less than the number of days in February.

64. INSPECTOR LOO AND THE STOLEN SUMMER

After a long stretch of solving crimes with swagger, gumshoe Commodius Loo was looking forward to a relaxing summer. He'd returned from a series of time-traveling adventures and planned to spend a month at a seaside inn near Northumberland. But alas, just before he boarded a train to the coast, duty called: the good inspector was recruited to serve as mentor to six young interns with big crime-solving dreams.

The interns had already worked on some cases, and before the inspector could get down to business, he needed to know how much experience each one had. The highest number of cases any intern had worked on was 10, and everyone had worked on at least two. They also had all worked on a different number of cases. Lucy Loo (the inspector's favorite niece) had seen twice as many cases as Michael Mastermind. Chris Clever had worked on four more cases than the next-ranked Guy Spy. Sherry Sherlock had seen two more cases than Dan Detective and one less than Guy Spy.

How many cases had each intern worked on already?

65. QUICK TRICK

Use each letter of the three words below once to spell out three types of trees.

CAMEL PEEL RUMPS

On the show *Hope and Faith,* actress Faith Ford played the character of Hope.

66. IN TWO STRAIGHT LINES...

It was time for the five kids in Mrs. Sawyer's class to line up for lunch. They could arrange themselves by height or age, and since Taylor was this week's class monitor and got to choose the way they lined up, she wanted to make sure she was near the front of the line. From these clues, can you put the kids in order by age and then by height so that Taylor can decide which gives her the best spot?

1. Taylor is the shortest.

2. Chandler is the tallest.

3. Payton is taller than David, but only by one place.

4. Jeff is taller than the only kid older than the only kid shorter than the only kid younger than Jeff.

67. SUBTRACTING UP

Can you figure out a way to take away 1 from 14 and end up with 15?

68. WORD SOUP

In column A, we've given you the first three letters of nine nine-letter words. In column B, you'll find the middle three letters, and in column C the last three letters. Each set includes letters in the proper order. Without rearranging any letters and by using each set of three letters only once, your job is to restore all the words.

A	B	C
TOU	KEB	OAT
ALB	VAN	GIC
NOS	CHD	OUS
MOT	UCI	IZE
SNA	IDA	OWN
EGR	ATR	ARY
FID	TAL	ITE
AFF	EGI	OSS
GAL	ORB	VIT

The Mall in Washington, D.C., is 1.4 times larger than Vatican City.

69. MATHEMATICAL MADNESS

Fill in the empty spots below using each number from 1 to 9 only once.

	−		x		=	5
+	■	x	■	x	■	■
	+		+		=	19
x	■	−	■	+	■	■
	−		x		=	48
=	■	=	■	=	■	■
63	■	15	■	41	■	■

70. WHAT'S A LITTLE DEATH AMONG FRIENDS?

Jack and Jay were on vacation when they crashed a swanky event at their hotel. Both men ordered glasses of gin on the rocks from the open bar, but as it turned out, the drinks they received were poisoned. (The party was a birthday celebration for a local mobster who'd been having trouble with a rival gang.) Jack drank his gin quickly and then headed out to a nearby nightclub, where he stayed, alive and well, for the rest of the evening. Jay remained at the party, sipped his gin, and dropped dead a short while later. How come one man lived and the other died?

71. IDIOMATIC IDIOSYNCRASIES

In this puzzle, the set of letters below represents the words of a popular English idiom. If CBARAAHP stands for "Caught between a rock and a hard place," what other well-known idiom do the following letters stand for? And what is the missing letter?

KTB_OS

Horned toads are actually lizards.

72. INTO THE WILD

Uncle John loves to hike, so on the first day of spring, he decided to make his own batch of trail mix for a weekend trek in the mountains. At the grocery store, he found that nuts cost 45 cents an ounce, raisins were 43 cents an ounce, and sunflower seeds were 36 cents an ounce. He bought enough to make a pound (16 ounces) of trail mix. As he checked out, he noticed that the total price of the ingredients meant his homemade trail mix would cost a reasonable 39 cents an ounce.

How many ounces each of nuts, raisins, and sunflower seeds did Uncle John buy?

73. SEQUENTIAL THINKING

What two letters come next in this series?

T F S E T T ? ?

74. MIRROR, MIRROR

A palindrome is a word or phrase that's spelled the same way backward and forward. The three palindromes below are missing some letters. What are the missing letters, and what words do they spell?

R _ _ A _ _ R

C _ _ _ C

_ E V E _

75. THE GREAT ESCAPE

Inspector Commodius Loo was trapped at the top of a castle in a chamber with no doors and only two windows. The first window led to a room filled with constantly boiling water, but it had a door at the far end that led out of the castle. The second window led to a room whose walls were made out of magnifying glass. It also had a door that led out of the castle, but when the sun shone through the glass, it burned everything in its path. Still, the inspector managed to save himself. How?

A pork butt roast comes from a pig's shoulder.

76. PHONE IT IN

Considering that...

ABC 2

DEF 3

GHI 4

JKL 5

MNO 6

PQRS 7

TUV 8

WXYZ 9

Use these phone numbers to spell out the last names of three famous people:

1. 256-6639

2. 742-8637

3. 946-3739

Odontophobia is the fear of teeth.

77. INSPECTOR LOO AND THE CASE OF THE BURGER JOINT BURGLARY

One afternoon, Inspector Commodius Loo was summoned to Big Bob's Burgers, where a gaggle of detectives was trying to solve a crime. Before Loo could flag anyone down, Officer John Tank was by his side.

"We've had this shop under surveillance for weeks," Tank said. "We thought someone was embezzling cash, but didn't know who, so we planted an agent on the inside. Problem is, no one ever told me who he was. So when I got down here and saw two guys fighting near the counter, I didn't know who to go after. The one in the blue shirt said the other one was the agent. And the one in the red shirt said the blue guy was the embezzler. I know that our agents never lie and embezzlers do, but I still didn't know who was who. I fired into the air, hoping that would stop them, but they both ran away. One went out the front door and the other one out the back."

Loo took a satisfied puff of his cigar and examined the scene: chairs and tables were upended, a pumpkin pie plate was cracked, and burger buns lay all over the floor. Tank's gun had recently been fired. Yet within minutes, Loo had ordered the other officers to make an arrest.

Whom did they cuff, and how did the good inspector solve the crime?

Sea moss mixed with milk and vanilla is a popular food in New Hampshire.

78. FRATERNAL TRIPLETS

To complete this puzzle, fill in the blanks with three words that differ by only one letter. The letter will be in the same position in all three words. Here's an example: The students had to _____ carefully to see when the new _____ of chicks would _____. Add "watch," "batch," and "hatch."

The ____ sparkled on the skaters in their fluffy ice-blue costumes and ice-blue ____ as they performed perfect figure ____.

79. WILD & WOOLLY WORDY

Can you figure out what word or phrase this stands for?

elin pu

80. ECHOES

What two homophones (words that sound alike but are spelled differently) are being described here?

Assessed a penalty for a great discovery

81. BACKWORDS

Read from right to left—there are two five-letter words hidden backward in the line of letters below. Do you see them?

W   Y   S   P   Y   G   L   A   S   E   V   E   R   E   K   O   J   B   A   N

82. YOU'RE GETTING WARMER

Changing one letter at a time, can you go from SNOW to RAIN in seven steps?

In Great Britain, royals get a 41-gun salute when they're born.

83. A PERFECT GUEST

After world-traveler Prendergast returned from his trip to Africa, he decided to write a book about his sometimes-harrowing experiences. One of the things he did to prepare for this was to make out lists of his discoveries. The following is an inventory of the hardships and pleasures he found at African hotels and their restaurants:

1. Where they serve antelope steak, the hotel restaurant employs only waitresses.

2. Year-round hotels serve huge tropical drinks.

3. They don't serve antelope steak at seedy hotels.

4. Hotels where waiters wear tuxedos are open only part of the year.

5. Hotels with swimming pools have elephants roaming nearby.

6. Seedy hotels don't allow pet chimpanzees.

7. Hotels without pools don't serve huge tropical drinks.

Are there any places where a chimpanzee fancier can watch elephants roam?

84. LETTER MASH

We've hidden six six-letter words in the grid below. Reading from left to right, choose one letter from each column to form the words. Each letter will be used only once.

T	I	R	A	N	Y
K	I	O	O	L	H
H	M	R	K	S	S
A	E	V	U	A	T
M	U	B	R	O	Y
R	O	M	L	E	O

Both *Father Knows Best* and *The Simpsons* took place in Springfield, state unknown.

85. TOP THIS

You just got a new job at Pete's Pizza Palace (congratulations!) and need to complete the menu board. But the guys there love wordplay and have their own system of pricing pizza toppings...and everyone's too busy to explain it to you. So you'll have to figure out on your own how much the pepperoni costs.

PETE'S PIZZA — PALACE —

MUSHROOMS	$13
GREEN PEPPERS	$7
SAUSAGE	$19
BLACK OLIVES	$2
PEPPERONI	?

The metal thing a pencil's eraser fits into is called a "shoulder."

86. LANDSCAPER LAND

Greener Pastures, a top-notch landscaping company, employs nine workers: Buzz, Abbott, Mark, Hank, Carlos, Tony, Vernon, Zack, and Dan. Their nine jobs are hole digger, planter, waterer, seeder, sodder, supervisor, and three mowers (reel mower, power mower, and rider mower).

1. Abbott, Zack, Hank, and the planter were once beaten at poker by the waterer.

2. Either Dan or Mark is a mower, but not both.

3. The seeder, the hole digger, and Hank like saunas.

4. Buzz and Tony married the waterer's sisters.

5. Abbott and Carlos often beat the sodder at canasta.

6. Among the sodder, planter, supervisor, hole digger, waterer, and seeder, only Carlos, Zack, and Mark have been with the company for more than five years.

7. The sodder married Hank's sister.

8. Buzz and the three mowers often shoot pool together. Abbott sometimes watches.

9. Mark is a very close friend of the planter.

10. Tony and Hank each weigh more than the supervisor.

11. Zack, Abbott, Mark, and the seeder drink beer after work.

12. The seeder, hole digger, waterer, and supervisor often go swimming with Zack and Carlos.

13. Tony and the power mower are best friends.

14. Mark used to work as both supervisor and waterer.

15. Dan likes to hang out at both the power mower's and reel mower's houses.

Who does what job?

87. LANGUAGE EQUATION

If "16 = O. in a P." stands for "16 ounces in a pound," what does this equation stand for?

$$18 = \text{H. on a G. C.}$$

88. WORD MYSTERY

Use the clues to figure out the mysterious word.

1. I am seven letters long.

2. Without 1 and 2, I'm an alternative.

3. My 1, 2, 3, 4, and 5 will keep you nourished.

4. But 2, 3, and 4 have gone bad.

5. Put all my letters together, and I may be part of your family.

What am I?

89. QUICK TRICK

Use each letter of the three words below once to spell out three types of automobiles.

ENCASE JUDO PEEP

90. RIDDLER

Inspector Commodius Loo found this classic riddle scribbled in the margin of one of his old schoolbooks:

> Black as night I'll always be,
> Until my mother smothers me.
> Then clear as ice I will become
> In the rough. Thank you, Mum!
> What am I?

91. MOTHER KNOWS BEST?

When Uncle John was a kid, his mother (Mama John) thought it was important to exercise her son's intellect. As a result, Uncle John was required to flex his mental muscles even when school was closed for vacations.

Over one winter holiday, Mama John typed up a list of 25 10-letter words and promised Uncle John that he'd get a pony for his birthday if he found all of the words in one issue of their town's weekly paper. Uncle John quickly came up with a solution that met his mother's challenge, freed up his vacation, and ensured that he'd get his pony.

How did he outsmart Mama John?

92. ADD 'EM UP

All of the numbers in the problem below (except the last two) have been replaced by letters. Can you figure out what numbers each letter represents so that the math is correct?

$$S I X + S I X = A 6 4$$

Australian farmers have to import beetles to eat dung their cow farms.

93. WORD SWAP

In each pair of words below, swap one letter from each to form two new words, while keeping the unswapped letters in the same sequence. For example, if the given pair were "spool" and "taste," the answers would be "stool" and "paste."

1. Great   Rate

2. Shame   Vane

3. Stoop   Wan

94. TRICK QUESTION

Uncle John asked everyone at the Bathroom Readers Institute the following questions, and only one person answered more than two correct. Only "yes" and "no" answers are allowed. Can you get more than two of these questions right?

1. Did Spain host the 2010 Winter Olympics?

2. Was George Washington the first U.S. president?

3. Is the answer to this question "yes"?

95. PILFERER OF PERSIA

Four ancient Persian potters—Aribis, Cacabil, Oothsez, and Daser—were traveling through the desert when two of them got into an argument about who was going to buy the day's beer. As a consequence, one of the squabbling potters stole the other one's prized gold glazing powder...and then disappeared.

The two who hadn't been robbed gave chase. Soon the pair ran into Inspector Commodius Loo, who was in ancient Persia doing a little time-traveling recon for an art heist back home. Loo assembled the facts below and easily deduced who the miscreant and victim were. He used these clues:

1. Cacabil was one of the potters who ran into Loo.

2. Daser had been sick to his stomach until the morning of the trip.

3. Oothsez wasn't the owner of the gold glazing powder, nor was he the thief.

4. The night before the trip, the potter whose glaze was stolen had dinner at the local caravanserai.

Who's the thief, and whose gold glazing powder did he steal?

96. TOOTHPICK ADDITION

Without breaking any of the toothpicks, move just one of them to make this equation correct. (Hint: Making a "not equal" sign is not the answer.)

97. SOLAR HIGH-JINKS

On the island of Oahu, Hawaii, the sun is almost 1,000 miles farther away at sunset than it is at noon. Why?

Technical name for a flower stem: *peduncle*.

98. INSIDE THE ACTORS' CLASSROOM

There are six high students in the Summerville High School film class. Their midterm exam consisted of three questions about actors during Hollywood's Golden Age. The students gave these answers:

1. Charlie Chaplin, Charlie Chaplin, Cary Grant

2. Cary Grant, Cary Grant, Charlie Chaplin

3. John Wayne, John Wayne, Charlie Chaplin

4. Cary Grant, Charlie Chaplin, John Wayne

5. John Wayne, Cary Grant, Cary Grant

6. Cary Grant, John Wayne, John Wayne

When the teacher graded the papers, he found that each student had answered at least one of the questions correctly. What are the correct answers to the three questions?

Charles Dickens's first job was labeling bottles of boot polish.

99. WILD & WOOLLY WORDY

Can you figure out what word or phrase this stands for?

Gives
Gives
Gives
Gives
Gets
Gets
Gets
Gets

100. SUM FUN!

Starting at the 3, add adjacent numbers by moving horizontally or vertically (but not diagonally) so that they total 37. You can use a number only once—no doubling back—and you won't necessarily use all the numbers.

6	1	3
2	8	4
7	9	5

It doesn't make sense: the Burnsi leopard frog has no spots.

101.
AND THE NUMBER IS...?

If a bottle full of water weighs 18 ounces and
the water weighs twice as much as the bottle,
how much does the bottle weigh?

102. READ BETWEEN THE LINES

The answer to each clue below includes the word "READ" at the beginning, the end, or in the middle of another word. For example, if the clue were "a decorative covering," the answer would be "bedspread." Can you identify these three things?

1. With the nap worn off.

2. A person between the ages of 9 and 12, generally.

3. An old tire that's been made like new.

103. BACKTRACKING

By reading backward, you can find at least four 4-letter words the given words. No fair changing the order of the letters, but you are allowed to skip over letters. Here's an example: in the word TENDER, you'll find RENT, but not REND.

How many can you identify?

1. TROOPSHIP

2. EVAPORATE

Don Corleone's phone number in *The Godfather*: Long Beach 4-5620.

104. BONUS PAY

Ben, Engelbert, and Flaherty were auto mechanics on their coffee break. When their boss passed by, he noticed that they all had grease smudges on their noses, and he decided to have some fun (and maybe win a few dollars).

"Men," he said, "I have a proposition for you. First, look at each other's noses and tell me if you see grease on them." The guys all nodded that they did. "Now," he continued, "I'll bet you fifteen dollars that none of you can tell me for sure that he has grease on his nose, or how and why he knows this."

Engelbert's hand went up in a flash. The boss's scheme was sunk. How did Engelbert find his way into the boss' wallet?

105. WILD & WOOLLY WORDY

Can you figure out what word or phrase this stands for?

J   O   H   N   S

Originally, "Quaker" was a derisive term. It was used to describe...

106. FRATERNAL TRIPLETS

To complete this puzzle, fill in the blanks with three words that differ by only one letter. The letter will be in the same position in all three words. Here's an example: The students had to _____ carefully to see when the new _____ of chicks would _____. Add "watch," "batch," and "hatch."

At the beginning of therapy, some patients tend to ____ because they ____ their negative feelings toward their shrinks, so the doctors have to work double-time to ____ the problem.

107. RAPID FIRE

• Two boys were born on the same day to the same mother, but they're not twins. How's that possible?

• Which of these words doesn't belong?
  AGE, POT, NOW, ATE

108. A CLOWN-UNDRUM

Plungy the Clown earned three gold bricks after working a children's birthday party. While walking home, he came to an old foot bridge. The sign said, "Weight Capacity: 150 pounds." Plungy weighed 148 pounds, and the three bricks weighed one pound each. How did he get across with all the gold?

Your intestinal lining covers twice the area that your skin does.

109. LANGUAGE EQUATION

If "16 = O. in a P." stands for "16 ounces in a pound," what does this equation stand for?

9 = I. in a B. G.

110. SAM LOYD CLASSIC: THE CASHIER'S PROBLEM

See if you can solve this classic by puzzle-maker extraordinaire Sam Loyd (1841–1911): Bank tellers run across some confusing math problems. For example, let's say you're a bank teller, and an old man came up to your window with a check for $200 and said, "Give me some one-dollar bills, ten times as many two-dollar bills, and the balance in fives!" What would you do?

111. IT'S SYMBOLIC

Put a mathematical symbol between the numbers 4 and 6 to get a number that's less than 6 but more than 4.

Only M*A*S*H movie cast member also on the TV show: Gary Burghoff (Radar).

112. THE PROVERB CODE

In the two common English proverbs below, we've changed all the letters except "S" and "Y": consonants are represented by the letter "B" and vowels by the letter "E." The punctuation is the same. What are the correct proverbs??

1. BE ES E SEY, BEB ES E BE.

2. E BEBBEBB SBEBE BEBBBEBS

BE BESS.

113. AT THE FAIR

Four farmers decided to take part in the livestock competition at this year's county fair. Based on these clues, can you figure out who brought which animals and where each person placed?

1. Amanda finished last, just behind the person who showed pigs.

2. The farmer who showed goats won the blue ribbon, and Annie came in second.

3. Annie and Charlie either showed goats and llamas (not necessarily in that order) or pigs and rabbits (not necessarily in that order).

4. Dustin didn't show goats or llamas.

114. BACKTRACKING

By reading backward, you can find at least four common four-letter words in the given words below. You may not change the order of the letters, but you are allowed to skip over letters. Here's an example: in the word TENDER, you'll find RENT, but not REND. How many can you identify?

1. PRAGMATIC
2. QUERULOUS

At least 25 states now offer traffic updates via Twitter.

115. NESTED WORDS

Like a set of nested eggs, this puzzle requires working from the outside in. First, find a synonym for the second phrase. Then, inside that new word, find a synonym for the first phrase. For example, if the puzzle were "a color in what a lender gives (3, 6)," the answer would be "'red' in 'credit.'" Now try this one:

To irritate in oddities (3, 6)

116. MATH TRICK

Here's a trick that's bound to amaze your friends—it amazes us! Get a calculator and type in the number 999,999. Divide it by 7. Next, choose a number between 1 and 6, and multiply your new number by that. Lastly, take the six digits in the answer and arrange them from lowest to highest. What do you have?

In the past 10,000 years, the human brain has shrunk by 10%.

117. THE VACATIONERS

Four friends—Winston, Theo, Mike, and Matt—decided to vacation at a resort outside of Sydney, Australia. They arrived on Sunday, Monday, Tuesday, and Wednesday, but not necessarily in that order. One of the vacationers was wearing a blue baseball cap, one had on a black sun visor, another sported brown flip-flops, and the fourth wore camo capris. Consider the following clues:

1. The two wearing headgear arrived on Sunday and Monday, and have twin sisters.

2. Only one person's first name begins with the same letter as the day he arrived.

3. Matt was not wearing the black sun visor.

4. The person who arrived on Wednesday and the one with the brown flip-flops have pet elephants.

5. Mike is an only child.

6. Winston was wearing the camo capris.

When did the guys arrive, and what were they wearing?

118. WILD & WOOLLY WORDY

Can you figure out what word or phrase this stands for?

CHANCE

119. MONEY TALKS

Uncle John loves fresh veggies, so last week, he took the day off and went to the new farmers' market in town. It was pricey, though, so he bought only one of each vegetable. He spent a total of $25. Carrots cost more than cucumbers. Green peppers cost more than twice as much as carrots. And one green pepper cost less than three cucumbers. How much did Uncle John spend on each vegetable?

120. MISSING NUMBERS

In the problem below, replace each question mark with either 1, 2, 3, or 4 to make the numbers add up correctly. Each number is used only once.

```
    ?   6   ?   7
    5   8   4   ?
+  _____
    7   ?   7   9
```

121. CURIOUS CONNECTIONS

It's not obvious, but these words have
something in common:

CHILLY

EFFORT

ACCEPT

FLOPPY

ALMOST

KNOTTY

GHOST

ACCENT

Figure out the connection, and then decide
which of these words belongs with those above.

GATHER

CHIMPS

FLINTY

SWEETS

CANINE

122. HE SHOULDA KNOWN BETTER

A con artist was sipping his mocha latte at a New Orleans café when he caught the eye of a tourist sitting next to him...and decided to score some pocket money off the guy. "See that couple two tables over?" the con artist asked as he sidled up to his mark. "Get this: their names are August and Marilyn, and they're married to each other. But I bet $100 that August has taken two trips to New Orleans with his wife Marilyn, even though Marilyn has come to New Orleans only once with her husband August." The mark was a born loser, so he took the bet. After a chat with Marilyn and August, the mark discovered that the grifter was telling the truth. But how could that be?

123. BACKWORDS

Read the line of letters below from right to left—there are two five-letter words hidden backward in them. Do you see the words?

N R E H S P A R K I K A H K I L E W O D

124. PARTY GAME

Last week, Uncle John corralled his dinner party guests into playing this game. He announced that five people would "be" the following animals: a salmon, cricket, ostrich, lion, and jumping spider. He secretly assigned each person one animal and told them to keep their animals a secret. Then he chose Gordon to be "it." Gordon got to ask only one question of the entire group to figure out who represented each animal, but he was not allowed to ask the obvious, "What animal are you?" So what should Gordon's question be?

125. TEASER

What's one way to drop a raw egg five feet over a concrete floor (with no cushioning) without breaking the egg?

126. OINK, OINK

These toothpicks below are arranged in the shape of a pig. Can you move two toothpicks so that the pig faces the opposite direction? (Don't overlap or break any toothpicks.)

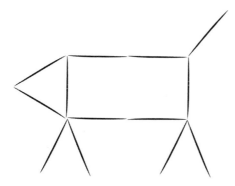

127. WORDPLAY

Can you think of an English word that starts with P
and whose pronunciation changes when its first letter
is capitalized?

128. FRATERNAL TRIPLETS

To complete this puzzle, fill in the blanks with three words
that differ by only one letter. The letter will be in the same
position in all three words. Here's an example: The students had to _____ carefully to see when the new _____
of chicks would _____. Add "watch," "batch," and "hatch."

"You spilled hot soup in my lap," the distraught restaurant patron ____ at the clumsy boy who ____ tables. But
the apologetic manager tore up the bill, and the soupy
diner finally ____ his threat to sue.

129. ABOVE OR BELOW?

The numbers below have been placed according to a particular rule. Can you figure out where 6 should go?

2   10
―――――――
3   7   8

130. A TRICKY GIFT

Ashley's father was very rich and very generous, but he also liked to have a little fun when he was distributing his wealth. So when he decided to give Ashley some gold for her birthday in November, he made a game of it. She could have one ounce each day for the 30 days of the month. Her present would be cut from a bar of gold that was 30 inches long and weighed 30 ounces. But there was another catch: her dad would do this only if Ashley could figure out the least number of pieces the bar could be cut into and still pay her an ounce a day.

She did it. How?

Dancing with the Stars judge Carrie Ann Inaba was an *In Living Color* "fly girl."

131. WATCH YOUR STEP

Changing one letter at a time, can you go from SHOE to BOOT in just three steps?

132. IDIOMATIC IDIOSYNCRASIES

In this puzzle, the set of letters below represents the words of a popular English idiom. If CBARAAHP stands for "Caught between a rock and a hard place," what other well-known idiom do the following letters stand for? And what is the missing letter?

TOTI_B

133. THINK ABOUT IT

Where is a day longer than a year?

"Nothing to me feels as good as laughing incredibly hard." —Steve Carell

134. QUOTE ME

Rearrange the anagrams in the brackets to figure out what Albert Einstein was trying to say.

"Any man who can drive safely while [A PIGLET RISKS TRYING] is simply not giving the [SKIS] the attention it deserves."
                    —Albert Einstein

135. MIRROR, MIRROR

A palindrome is a word or phrase that's spelled the same way backward and forward. The three palindromes below are missing some letters. Can you figure out what they are and spell the right word or phrase?

_ O _ O _

R _ F _ R

_ _ D D _ _

136. BACK TO SCHOOL

Last month, Anna's high school hosted Back to School Week, in which family members could visit a student's classes, meet teachers, and tour the school. Anna's mom, dad, and Aunt Sue all wanted to go, but...

1. None of the family members could visit Anna's school on the same day.

2. Each attended a different class's presentation on Monday, Tuesday, or Wednesday.

3. The math class visitation was scheduled two days before the one for the English class.

4. Aunt Sue was out of town for two presentations before the one she attended.

5. Mom went to the science presentation.

Which family member went to which class on what day?

137. LANGUAGE EQUATION

If "16 = O. in a P." stands for "16 ounces in a pound," what does this equation stand for?

$$1 = G. L. for M.$$

138. POCKET CHANGE

You've got a pocketful of U.S. coins (none of them are dollars), but your friends are frustrated—you can't make them exact change for a nickel, a dime, a quarter, a 50-cent piece, or a dollar. What's the maximum amount of money you can have in your pocket for this situation to be true?

139. WILD & WOOLLY WORDY

Can you figure out what word or phrase this stands for?

$$P ^A Y$$

A "welterweight" boxer must weigh between 140 and 147 pounds.

140. WHAT ARE THE ODDS?

In a card game like Spades or Bridge—in which all the cards are dealt to four players at the beginning of the game—what's more likely: that you and your partner would be dealt all the cards in one suit, or that you'd get none of the cards in one suit?

141. CLASSROOM ANTICS

Subterfuge Secondary School has only two classrooms: one large and one small. On the days that they meet in the large classroom, the girls always tell the truth and the boys always lie. When they meet in the small classroom, it's exactly the opposite: the girls lie, and the boys tell the truth.

One day, two students—a boy from the large classroom and a student from the small classroom—met in the hallway. Sam said, "You and I are both boys." Morgan said, "You and I are different genders."

Who's telling the truth?

142. P-P-P-POKER CHIPS

Take a look at the flower-shaped poker chips below. Each one is worth $10. The way they're arranged now, they create three straight lines (vertically, horizontally, and diagonally), each of which contains three chips. Your job is to move just one chip so that the arrangement meets the criteria below.

- You've got at least two straight lines that contain at least three chips.
- Each line totals $40 in chips.

(Hint: There are three possible ways to solve this. Can you find all three?)

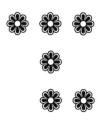

143. TELLING TIME

If it were two hours from now, it would be half as long until 8:00 p.m. as it would be an hour from now. What time is it?

144. THIS OR THAT

What word fits both definitions?

"A unit of measurement" and "an enclosed piece of land"

145. BACKWORDS

Read from right to left—there are two five-letter words hidden backward in the line of letters below. Do you see them?

D E R H S A L V Y M A P L E C X E N O N

Female sharks lose their appetite while giving birth so they won't eat their young.

146. ANAGRAM THIS

An anagram is a word or phrase that's formed by rearranging the letters of another word or phrase. For example, "MEAT" can be rearranged to get "TAME" or "MATE." What common 10-letter words can you make with these anagrams?

DECAF TOFUS

EDICT SIREN

COSMIC PORE

147. RAPID FIRE

• Unscramble these nine letters: A C C E H I M N S. What two words do they spell?

• There's one letter that doesn't appear in the name of any U.S. state. What is it?

Largest freshwater fish ever caught: a giant catfish in Thailand in 2005 (646 pounds).

148. A SWELL SUMMER VACATION

Three members of the Moneybags family—Mr., Mrs., and Junior—wanted to beat the summer heat by getting out of town. They came up with three jet-setting destinations (Rome, London, and Paris), but couldn't agree on which one to visit. So after much arguing—and much pouting from Junior—they finally decided to do away with family time and holiday on their own. Each Moneybags family member left on the same afternoon, but they used three different kinds of transportation (boat, plane, and train) and departed at three different times: 2:05, 2:19, and 3:32.

1. The three destinations were Paris, the place accessed by train, and the place whose transportation departed at 2:05.

2. Junior Moneybags left before the person who went to London.

3. The boat hadn't yet left when Mrs. Moneybags departed.

4. Mr. Moneybags did not go to Paris.

Given these clues, can you figure out when each person left, where he or she went, and by what method of transportation?

149. ECHOES

What two homophones (words that sound alike but are spelled differently) are being described here?

A dog's feet stop

150. IT ALL ADDS UP

One rainy day, Jenny was snooping around in her grandmother's hope chest. No one had looked in there since Grandma was a girl, and to Jenny's delight, she found six wrinkled bills at the very bottom. None of them were $1 bills, and they totaled $63. What were the denominations?

151. WEEKLY WONDERINGS

Name three days of the week without saying Sunday, Monday, Tuesday, Wednesday, Thursday, Friday, or Saturday.

...the *chushkopek*—an appliance that can roast seven peppers at once.

152. PHONE IT IN

Considering that...

ABC 2

DEF 3

GHI 4

JKL 5

MNO 6

PQRS 7

TUV 8

WXYZ 9

Use these phone numbers to spell out the last names of three famous people:

1. 773-7539

2. 536-6339

3. 254-6866

By 2009, only a third of Hollywood movies were shot in California.

153. INSPECTOR LOO AND THE FINE ART OF DETECTION

Between sips of Guinness at Copper's Tavern, Inspector Commodius Loo was waxing poetic on the finer points of the detecting trade. During these informal seminars, the good inspector often lapsed into an almost trancelike state. In this condition, he often spoke in the strange tongue of anagrammology, in which even the most ordinary words emerged in garbled mutations.

"Take your typical SCREEN MICE," he said. "You'll find it crawling with COIF REFS. I myself have often seen FERN STRIPING all over the place, not to mention numerous suspicious PROFIT SNOT on the ground."

"What do you do with those?" a rookie cop asked.

"Send them to the CABLE RIM, of course," said Loo. "And don't forget to look for CREVICED TEENA. You might need to take a PET ART CLASS."

"What about skid marks?" asked another cop.

"You have to preserve those. Use an aerosol resin to fix them in place, although you can also use AIRY HARPS."

Coming out of his near-trance, Inspector Loo looked at his watch. "Time to be heading out there, lads," he said. "I leave you with one final thought. Don't forget where you heard this... COOL POINTERS!"

Can you translate the nine anagrammed terms?

154. MIXED MESSAGE

The seven letters below can be rearranged into several other seven-letter words. Use each letter only once to make each new word. How many can you find?

A   E   I   L   R   S   T

155. SEQUENTIAL THINKING

What number comes next in this series?

423 654 236 542 ?

156. LANGUAGE EQUATION

If "16 = O. in a P." stands for "16 ounces in a pound," what does this equation stand for?

100 = S. in C.

Three out of four people have at least one wart.

157. NESTED WORDS

Like a set of nested eggs, this puzzle requires working from the outside in. First, find a synonym for the second phrase. Then, inside that new word, find a synonym for the first phrase. For example, if the puzzle were "a color in what a lender gives (3, 6)," the answer would be "'red' in 'credit.'" Now try this one:

A primate in a material made of cellulose pulp (3, 5)

158. SUM FUN!

What number does each letter represent?

$$A\ A\ A\ A$$

$$B\ B\ B\ B$$

$$+\ C\ C\ C\ C$$

$$\overline{A\ B\ B\ B\ C}$$

159. AND THE AGES ARE...

Thom has three daughters: Two of them are identical twins. The product of their ages is 36, and the eldest one has blue eyes. How old is each of Thom's kids?

160. ALL OR SOME?

If all Biggles are Piggles and no Piggles are Giggles, which of the following is true?

      a. All Biggles are Giggles

      b. No Biggles are Giggles

      c. Some Biggles are Giggles

      d. Can't tell

161. BACKWORDS

Read from right to left—there are two five-letter words hidden backward in the line of letters below. Do you see them?

B E R E T H C A Y P H R O O L G I Z M O

162. SEQUENTIAL THINKING

What should come next on this list of states?

> Vermont
>
> Connecticut
>
> Virginia
>
> Tennessee
>
> New York
>
> Kentucky
>
> Indiana

163. ANALOGY LESSON

KAYAK is to LION OIL as RACECAR is to _____?

> **a.** CAT TAIL
>
> **b.** JUMP START
>
> **c.** RAT STAR
>
> **d.** POP TOP

Oscar the Grouch was originally yellow...then orange...then green.

164. THE ALL-NEW ADVENTURES OF SUPERMOM

Jennifer Extraordinaire (supermom to one set of septuplets and one set of triplets) was trying to corral her kids into a line so they could all walk home from the candy store. The kids always stood in the same order—that way, Jennifer knew everyone was accounted for. But today, they were all hopped up on sugar and seemed to have forgotten their places. Here's how they were supposed to stand:

1. Sally should be behind Joe and Sam, but ahead of Pete and Ali.

2. Ali should be ahead of Callie.

3. Callie should be ahead of Tally, but behind Moe, Poe, and Sally.

4. Poe should be ahead of Tally, Sam, and Hallie.

5. Hallie should be ahead of Sally, Sam, and Pete.

6. Joe should be behind Moe and Poe.

7. Moe and Joe should be ahead of Callie.

8. Pete should be behind Sam, Tally, and Sally.

9. Sam should be ahead of Ali, Joe, and Moe.

Can you put all of Jennifer's kids in order, from first to last?

165. STARRY, STARRY PUZZLE

How many rectangles use four of these stars as corners?

166. SWEET TOOTH

All of Joan's jelly beans are yellow, except for two. All of them are blue, except for two. And all of them are green, except for two. How can this be?

The queen of England can't enter the House of Commons—she's not a commoner.

167. QUICK TRICK

Move one number to make this equation correct:

$$101 - 102 = 1$$

168. WILD & WOOLLY WORDY

Can you figure out what word or phrase this stands for?

MbYeWhOiRnKd

169. ECHOES

What two homophones (words that sound alike but are spelled differently) are being described here?

Autry's pants

170. THE SPACE COWBOYS

In the year 2315, a group of intergalactic cowboys (all from different spaceships) gathered at a bar near Jupiter for a little R&R. They were drinking heavily and playing a tense hand of Sagittarian Stud.

1. The cowboy from the *Endeavor* won the most money but didn't drink scotch.

2. The cowboy from the *Intrepid* was a loser, but not the biggest loser.

3. Tumbleweed Ted was not from the *Traveler*, and Jesse wasn't from the *Galileo*.

4. The cowboy who drank gin lost $4,000, and Frank won $1,000.

5. Bronco Billy didn't drink scotch or beer, and he won $1,000 less than Duke.

6. The cowboy from the *Traveler* lost the most money.

7. Duke won $3,000...$5,000 more than the whiskey drinker, who was a loser.

8. The cowboy from the *Pegasus* won the third-largest amount of money.

9. The bourbon drinker ordered everyone a round of shots.

Can you figure out what each cowboy was drinking, what ship he was from, and how much money he won or lost?

171. A BERRY GOOD PUZZLE

Hoppy the hobo was drifting through the countryside when he spied a strawberry farm. He was hungry, so he swiped as many berries as he could carry in his pockets. Suddenly, the farmer and his two sons appeared. Hoppy was caught red-handed and, with no way to explain himself, did the first thing that came to mind: he gave the farmer half of the loot.

Then he gave one son half of the remaining berries, and the other son half the berries left after that. To be on the safe side, he gave all three of them one more berry apiece. There were only two berries left, and the farmer, in his generosity, let Hoppy keep those.

How many berries did the hobo give back?

172. A CLASSIC

Let's say you've got two clocks. One loses a minute every day. One doesn't work at all. Which one is more accurate?

173. WHAT'S MISSING?

Take a look at the four vertical sets of numbers below and see if you can figure out what the missing number is.

$$
\begin{array}{cccc}
4 & 2 & 8 & 9 \\
2 & 1 & 7 & 6 \\
4 & 2 & 6 & 9 \\
4 & ? & 2 & 3
\end{array}
$$

174. RIDDLER

Going forward, I'm heavy, but going backward, I'm not. What am I?

...of the food depicted have increased by 69%.

175. FRATERNAL TRIPLETS

To complete this puzzle, fill in the blanks with three words that differ by only one letter. The letter will be in the same position in all three words. Here's an example: The students had to _____ carefully to see when the new _____ of chicks would _____. Add "watch," "batch," and "hatch."

The lifeguard had ____ out since last summer, and he ____ bright pink when he ____ on how gross he was going to look in a skimpy bathing suit.

176. WORD MYSTERY

Use the clues to figure out the mysterious word.

1. I am seven letters long.

2. My 1, 2, and 3 will keep your head warm.

3. But without 1, 2, and 4, it really hurts.

4. My 1, 5, and 7 are a positive verb.

5. Put all my letters together, and I'm running the ship.

What am I?

Turkeys can have stress-induced heart attacks.

177. MAKING THE SCENE

Three fashionable friends went out for a night on the town. Normally, they disagreed about everything, but tonight they settled on the Local Yokel, a watering hole known for its elegantly limited menu. Even more astonishingly, they all agreed to order one meal from the following choices and share it: Main courses were hot dogs Canadian, chicken à la king, and fried clams. The available desserts were a hot-fudge sundae, banana cream pie, and mint cookies. However, the ordering was made difficult by the following facts:

1. Stew hates fried clams, and he won't follow hot dogs with a hot-fudge sundae.

2. Clara won't eat hot dogs with banana cream pie, or a hot-fudge sundae if the main course is chicken à la king.

3. Bertram will eat chicken à la king only if it is followed by a hot-fudge sundae.

What did the friends have for dinner?

178. ELEPHANT RIDE

Using a very light crane, Arthur the circus wrangler needed to raise an elephant from the ground to a helicopter hovering 25 feet above. But every time Arthur pulled the elephant up 10 feet, it slipped back 5 feet. When the beast finally got to the helicopter, how many feet had it traveled altogether?

179. COUNT 'EM

How many 8s are there between 1 and 100?

180. HIDDEN WORDS

How many shorter common words can you find hiding in the long word below by reading from left to right? For example, IMPERSONATORS includes the words imp, per, person, son, on, at, etc. Can you find at least 10 words in this one? (One-letter words like "I" and "A" don't count.)

DISCONCERTING

The movie *Abbott and Costello Go to Mars* takes place on Venus.

181. SPLIT CITIES

Seven U.S. capital cities have been cut in half. Your mission, should you choose to accept it, is to put them back together. (Hint: Each city has six letters, but one set of three letters isn't used.)

PIE	TOP	BOS
ENA	DEN	HEL
ANY	NTO	RRE
EKA	TON	ALB
TIN	VER	AUS

182. LANGUAGE EQUATION

If "16 = O. in a P." stands for "16 ounces in a pound," what does this equation stand for?

$$4 = Q. \text{ in a } F. G.$$

183. A COLORFUL OUTING

Once a week at Manny's Marvelous Adventure Emporium, there's a grand paintball battle among the most skilled warriors. This week, the heroes shot their signature colors (blue, red, yellow, and brown). They also wore camo fatigues in those colors, but each hero's outfit was not necessarily the same color as his or her paintballs.

1. Arlo was the only combatant whose fatigues were the same color as the paint he shot.

2. Howard was not wearing a red or blue outfit.

3. Allan shot blue paintballs.

4. The battler in the brown fatigues shot yellow ammo.

5. Rhonda did not shoot red paintballs and did not wear yellow.

What color paintballs did each warrior employ, and what color was his or her camo before it was covered with paint?

184. THROW AWAY THE KEY!

Changing one letter at a time, can you go from TALE to JAIL in three steps?

To *hebetate* is to become boring or stupid.

185. ANAGRAMMIT

An anagram is a word or phrase that's formed by rearranging the letters of another word or phrase. For example, "meat" can be rearranged to get "tame" or "mate." What common 10-letter words can you make with these anagrams?

MADMEN STIR

A SQUINT TOO

HALCYON ELM

186. EXTREME MAKEOVER: LOGIC PUZZLE EDITION

It's house-building time, and the race is on. Four moms can build a house as fast as five dads. Two dads and one mom can build a house as fast as one kid. So if one kid and two dads team up against four moms, who will win?

187. LIAR, LIAR, PANTS ON FIRE!

Graffiti High School was a tough place, so Principal Riggs wasn't surprised when three students suspected of spray-painting the walls in the cafeteria were brought to him. All the students were boys, but only one could be the culprit. Riggs knew from experience that the malefactor would certainly lie, and the innocent boy would tell the truth.

The first boy Riggs questioned mumbled something that might have been nasty. The second boy pointed at the first and said, "We didn't do it." The third one pointed at the second and sneered, "He's a liar."

From this, Principal Riggs instantly knew who was the worst of the bad apples. How did he figure it out?

188. THE CLEVER SERVANTS

Robert, Brian, and Jiggs have been employees at Lord Chesterfield's manor for varying lengths of time. In fact, it had been so long that the men had forgotten who was the first to be employed. They knew, however, that Robert had one-third more years of service than Brian, and Jiggs had one-third as many as Robert. Together they have given 74 years of service to Lord Chesterfield. How many years does each man have?

189. SQUARE PEGS

In front of you is a wooden board with four round holes set up like coordinates on a map (north, east, south, and west). In each hole is a painted peg labeled A, B, C, or D, but not necessarily in that order. Here's what we know:

1. The A peg is painted red and is in the north hole.

2. The B peg is to the left of the C peg.

3. The peg painted green isn't C, and the yellow peg isn't D.

4. The blue peg is directly across from the yellow one.

In what hole is each lettered peg, and what color are the pegs?

190. CHAIN REACTION

Insert a word between the two given words to create two new words. For example, adding GUN between BLOW and POWDER would produce BLOWGUN and GUNPOWDER.

BOUNTY _____ GREEN

FINAL _____ SQUARE

191. TREED

Some people are just naturally good at clambering around the old family tree and figuring out the complex relationships among individuals. (Others are content with sitting around the trunk drinking lemonade.) Which group are you in?

Can you figure out what relation to you these family members would be?

    1. Your aunt's mother's only grandchild

    2. Your aunt's father's mother's husband

    3. Your mother's aunt's brother's wife

192. BACKTRACKING

By reading backward, you can find at least four four-letter words in the given words. No fair changing the order of the letters, but you are allowed to skip over letters. Here's an example: in the word TENDER, you'll find RENT, but not REND. How many can you identify?

    1. REBELLIONS

    2. SEASONABLE

193. SAM LOYD CLASSIC: A TRICKY PROBLEM

See if you can solve this classic by puzzle-maker extraordinaire Sam Loyd (1841–1911): Write down five odd numerals that add up to 14.

194. GUESS WHO'S NOT COMING TO DINNER?

A man arrives home from a day on the golf course, checks on the dog, walks through the living room, and glances toward his wife, who has had a heart attack. Then he goes to the kitchen, picks up the phone, calls Lefty's Lucky Pizza Delivery, and orders an extra-large pie with anchovies. Is he an insensitive jerk?

195. MOON OVER IT

If a full moon happens every 28.75 days, is it possible to see two full moons in one month and no full moons in another?

196. DELI DELIGHTS

The guys at Dave's Deli love wordplay, and they've devised a devious system to determine the prices of their sandwiches. Using their numbers, figure out their system to come up with the price of a BLT.

DAVE'S DELI

CORNED BEEF $42

PASTRAMI $33

TUNA SALAD $39

HAM & CHEESE $39

BLT ....?

A German shepherd's carbon footprint is three times that of the average SUV.

197. WHAT'S NEXT?

What should come next in this sequence of numbers?

1234
1603
1972
2341
2710
?

198. SHOPPING SPREE

Beth and Lisa were shopping at Bloomingsale's but didn't pay attention to the time and got locked in overnight. Luckily, they found a flashlight, a pen, and a small magazine of puzzles that a bored sales clerk left behind. Not so luckily, most of the puzzles had already been completed, and the women quickly solved the rest. But then Beth (ever resourceful) handed Lisa the magazine and asked her to tear out a page—without saying which one it was, of course.

Next, Beth told Lisa to add up the remaining page numbers and tell her the total. When Lisa said that the total was 90, Beth did some figuring in her head. After a while, she announced that she knew what page numbers appeared on the page Lisa had torn out and how many pages were originally in the magazine. What were they?

American plastic surgeons remove about 5,469 feet of noses each year.

199. THE FORGETFUL RACING FAN

Manny bet money on six horses in one race. One of them came in first, but Manny forgot which one. Luckily, he recalled five important facts. Can you help him sort them out and identify the winner?

1. Bonehead finished four lengths behind Valiant.

2. Valiant finished three lengths ahead of Moondog.

3. Moondog finished six lengths behind Caveman.

4. Caveman finished one length ahead of Monster.

5. Tessie tied with Valiant.

200. WORDPLAY

Besides the fact that the words below begin with silent letters, they have something else in common. What is it?

Scent Gnu   Hour
Knot   Aisle Whole

201. CONNECTIONS

The five words below have something in common.
What is it?

ADAM, BUOY, CLAIM, GALL, RAMP

202. WILD & WOOLLY WORDY

Can you figure out what word or phrase this stands for?

LE̸AST

203. SEQUENTIAL THINKING

What number comes next in this series? (Hint: This isn't a "number" puzzle.)

2 3 4 6 7 8 10 11 12 13 14 16 ?

204. THE MAGIC SQUARE

Benjamin Franklin—scientist, inventor, diplomat, author, printer, and Founding Father—was also a mathematician. As a young man, he devised the 8 x 8 magic square below, using the numbers from 1 to 64. What's a magic square? It's a square in which the numbers in all the rows, columns, and diagonals add up to the same amount. In the case of Franklin's, the magic number is 260. But there's more: Ben Franklin's magic square has at least seven other unique mathematical things about it. Can you identify them?

52	61	4	13	20	29	36	45
14	3	62	51	46	35	30	19
53	60	5	12	21	28	37	44
11	6	59	54	43	38	27	22
55	58	7	10	23	26	39	42
9	8	57	56	41	40	25	24
50	63	2	15	18	31	34	47
16	1	64	49	48	33	32	17

Length of vocal cords at birth: 2.5". Length at age 30: 12" for men, 8" for women.

205. HEY, SPORTS FANS

What timeless game allows offensive players to score without ever touching the ball and defensive players to maintain possession of the ball?

206. LANGUAGE EQUATION

If "16 = O. in a P." stands for "16 ounces in a pound," what does this equation stand for?

5 = D. in a Z. C.

207. KNOW WHEN TO HOLD 'EM

We've laid out three cards below. One of them is a Jack, which is just to the right of a three. A Jack is also just to the left of a Jack. A diamond is just to the right of a diamond, and a diamond is just to the left of a heart. What are the cards?

208. GRANDMOTHER TIME

Darla, a bright girl of middle-school age, was doing a homework biography of her grandmother Agnes, who had devoted her working life to numbers.

When Darla asked Agnes for a summary of her life, Grandma couldn't resist putting it in the form of a math problem.)

Agnes said, "After I was born, I spent the first one-fourth of my life in Nebraska. For the next one-sixth of my life, I lived in Texas working as an accountant. Immediately after that, I moved to Delaware, where I was a math teacher for the next one-third of my life, followed by 12 years in Georgia, where I was a college professor. Then I retired and moved to Minnesota, where I've now lived for the last one-twelfth of my life. How old am I now?"

What did Darla come up with?

209. ECHOES

What two homophones (words that sound alike but are spelled differently) are being described here?

Nasty demeanor

210. WORD MYSTERY

Use the clues to figure out the mysterious word.

1. I am seven letters long.

2. My 1, 3, 4, and 5 will keep your money safe.

3. Without 6 and 7, I'm pretty dull.

4. My 3 and 7 turn me into a preposition.

5. Put all my letters together, and I can keep you warm.

What am I?

211. THINK ON IT

One day last winter, when the power went out and he was stuck at home, Uncle John started thinking of words that use two Vs in a row. He came up with five common words. How many can you name?

212. NUMBER FUN

Use the clues below to fill in the grid with the numbers 1 through 9. Each number is used only once, and we've given you one digit to get you started.

1. The last two vertical columns and the diagonal row labeled B add up to the same amount.

2. In each of the first two vertical columns, no consonants are repeated in each column if you spell out the numbers. In the last column, the letter N shows up more than once if the numbers are spelled out.

3. The diagonal row labeled A adds up to 16.

A   **B**

1   ?   ?

?   ?   ?

?   ?   ?

Best-selling musical act that isn't American or British: AC/DC of Australia.

213. WATCH OUT!

Peter was seated—but not on solid ground—and writing when a thunderstorm struck and he was killed. What was he doing, and how did he die?

214. BONES OF CONTENTION

Three talking dogs found 24 bones. Purely by chance, each dog got the number of bones that was equal to his age three years ago. But the dogs were different ages, so they didn't all get the same number of bones. The youngest (and smartest) dog suggested a way for each of them to end up with the same number of bones.

"I will keep only half the bones I got," he said, "and you two can divide the rest equally. But then the middle dog, keeping half of his bones, has to divide the rest equally between the oldest dog and me. Then the oldest dog has to divide his equally between the middle dog and me."

They agreed, and each dog wound up with eight bones. How old were the dogs?

215. A TRIP DOWN LIAR'S LANE

In a very unusual town is a street called Liar's Lane—it starts at the top of a hill and winds down to the bottom. Many houses line the street, but only members of two families reside in them: the Joneses and the Smiths. The Joneses always tell the truth, and the Smiths always lie...but only if they live at the top of the hill. Smiths and Joneses who live at the bottom of the hill do exactly the opposite.

One day, two residents of Liar's Lane made the following statements: John said, "Scott lives at the top of the hill." Scott said, "John lives at the bottom of the hill." Then John said, "Scott's last name is Smith." Scott said, "John's last name is Jones."

Who's lying, where is each man actually from, and what's his last name?

216. TRICKY MATH

Is it possible for 6 + 24 = 1 to be correct? Maybe not in math class, but when it's written like this, it certainly is: 6 days + 24 hours = 1 week. See if you can figure out the problem below in a similar fashion.

$$4 + 1 = 1$$

Japan has more roads than Canada.

217. THE DISASTROUS DERBY

Three friends spent their Sunday blowing money at the Disastrous Derby (a horse race for rejects). Eight horses were racing that afternoon, but they only ran in races of two. The friends made bets on those four matches. Their choices, in no particular order, were as follows:

1. Bud chose Badly Bred, Chokes Before Finish, Trail Ride, and Lame-o to win.

2. Brad bet on Lags Behind, Trail Ride, Slow Poke, and Badly Bred.

3. Byron picked Lame-o, Badly Bred, Sir Cries a Lot, and Slow Poke.

4. No one bet on Break a Leg.

In the end, each friend picked only one winner. Which horses won?

218. MOMMY AND ME

Five moms met at the park for a playdate. Along the
fence, they lined up their five colored strollers: pink, purple, green, blue, and yellow, in that order from left to right.
Each of the kids (Pebbles, Bootsy, Caitlin, Michael, and
Bo) was wearing a different piece of clothing: a T-shirt, a
onesie, a baseball cap, soft shoes, or a bib. And the five
moms (Laura, Jane, Susan, Joanne, and Bonnie) were
chatting together on a bench, watching the kids play.
When it was time to go, the moms collected their kids
and put them into the strollers.

1. Bo was sitting next to the kid who wore the
onesie and the kid whose mom is Joanne.

2. Laura, Bonnie, and Jane didn't put their
strollers next to each other's, and none of them is
mom to the kid in the T-shirt.

3. There are at least two strollers between Susan's
kid and Bootsy.

4. The kid who wears the baseball cap does not sit
next to Joanne's kid, and is two or three strollers
to the right of the kid in the bib.

5. Caitlin sits to the right of Michael and to the left
of Jane's kid.

6. Bonnie's kid is not in the pink stroller.

Can you figure out which kid sits in which stroller,
what each child is wearing, and who is mom to whom?

219. BACKWORDS

Read from right to left—there are two five-letter words hidden backward in the line of letters below. Do you see them?

U P S A R T Y A T O U Q U I R E V O C S

220. DYNAMIC TRIOS

We've removed all the consonants from the pairs of words below, but the pairs have something in common. What is the common thread, and what consonants are missing? (To help you out, we put the list of pairs in alphabetical order.)

1. A _ _ O _ _ & _ _ E O _ A _ _ A

2. _ A _ _ I E & _ E N

3. _ _ A _   _ I _ _ & A _ _ E _ I _ A   _ O _ I E

221. GENDER ROLES

Can you identify the only suffix used in English to make a feminine word masculine?

222. SEQUENTIAL THINKING

What number should come next in this series?

1, 3, 12, 60, 360, ?

223. ECHOES

What two homophones (words that sound alike but are spelled differently) are being described here?

Workers on an ocean liner

224. MONEY TALKS

There's $16 on the table in front of you: a $1 bill, a $5 bill, and a $10 bill. If you say something that's true, you might get one of the bills. If you say something untrue, though, you'll get nothing. What can you say to make sure you walk away with the $10?

225. WILD & WOOLLY WORDY

Can you figure out what word or phrase this stands for?

THE RI   THE POORCH

226. YIKES!

Andy is riding a horse. Directly to his left is a tiger traveling at the same speed. In front of him is an elephant, also traveling at the same speed. Right behind him—at the same speed—is a lion. And to his right is a ledge. How can Andy make it to safety?

227. FRATERNAL TRIPLETS

To complete this puzzle, fill in the blanks with three words that differ by only one letter. The letter will be in the same position in all three words. Here's an example: The students had to _____ carefully to see when the new _____ of chicks would _____. Add "watch," "batch," and "hatch."

"I can't create when I have unhappy workers around me," said the famous ____ to his new assistant. "So please wipe that ____ off your face, or I'll have to fire you and you'll have to find another ____."

228. THREES PLEASE

Use addition, subtraction, multiplication, or division to make these equations correct. All you have to do is insert the right symbols.

1. 3 3 3 3 3 = 24
2. 3 3 3 3 3 = 0
3. 3 3 3 3 3 = 6

229. INSPECTOR LOO AND THE INTERRUPTED STROLL

Spring had finally sprung, and Inspector Commodius Loo ambled past his neighborhood park, his fedora tipped slightly to one side and humming a jaunty tune. He stopped for a moment to smell the roses and watch the traffic go by. Three cars, a chartered bus, and a motorcycle sped up to make it through a yellow light, bumping over the railroad tracks as they went.

Just then a siren blared toward him, and Loo's cell phone rang. It was Headquarters.

"Loo," the dispatcher gabbled. "We've got a report of a break-in at Chestnut and Lancaster. GPS shows that you're just around the corner. Did you see anything suspicious?"

The good inspector straightened his hat as a police car roared by.

"I did indeed," he declared. "You should be looking for the thieves to be escaping in a chartered bus."

Sure enough, just a few miles down the road, police officers arrested the criminals as they were abandoning their bus and heading for the woods. How did Loo solve the crime?

230. COIN TOSS

Adam and Joe each flipped a coin 20 times. Joe got 14 heads and 6 tails, but Adam got heads every time. What are the chances that Adam will get heads on his 21st coin toss?

231. CLASSIC

What is cowhide most often used for?

232. UP AND DOWN

Angela was painting the eaves of her house, and she was standing on a ladder propped against the side. She started on the middle rung and went up six, then down eight, up three, and up eight more to reach the top. How many rungs were on the ladder?

The first animal to live on land: the scorpion, about 440 million years ago.

233. DIGITAL ARCHITECTURE

The Flushing Hotel is a very tall building. In fact, it's so tall that the number of floors is three digits, with each digit being larger than the one preceding it. It came to have that number of floors in the following way: The architect made a bet with his secretary. If she could tell him a number—which had a difference between the sum of its digits and the product of its digits that fell between (and might include) 0 and 10—he would make the building that number of floors, and she would get a $25 bonus. If she lost, she owed him lunch. She won. What is the magic number?

234. PREFERENCES

Uncle John likes 25 but not 26, 196 but not 195, and 100 but not 99. Does he prefer 63 or 64?

235. MATH CIPHER

All of the numbers in the equation below have been
replaced by letters. What letters represent what numbers
(0–9) to make the six equations correct? (Each number is
used at least once.)

$$ARJF - FGQ = AAJC$$
$$\div \qquad - \qquad -$$
$$RH + FQF = HAC$$
$$\overline{}$$
$$HR \times FC = BCP$$

236. LET'S PLAY CARDS

We've hidden six card games in the string of letters below.
To find them, you'll need to take groups of consecutive
letters (from left to right) and rearrange them to get the
names of the games. Letters may overlap between words,
but you won't reuse any letter in a single word. For example, the first five letters spell "rummy." Can you find the
other five games?

R Y M U M T O L R S E A I I N G D B E I R S D A E P S T E A R H

237. WORD FIND

What English word meets these criteria?

1. It's nine letters long.

2. It contains three As, two Gs, one R, one T, one additional vowel, and one additional consonant.

238. WILD & WOOLLY WORDY

Can you figure out what word or phrase this stands for?

SOEBULD TENNIS

239. I'LL BET YA

Two-eff Jeff was sitting in a chair in the center of a room. One-eff Jef walked up and said, "I'll bet you a dollar that before I run around your chair three times, you'll get up." Two-eff Jeff took the bet, sure he'd make an easy buck, but when all was said and done, One-eff Jef won. How?

Grapefruit are so named because, like grapes, they grow in clusters.

240. A NUMBERS GAME

Arrange the numbers 7, 8, 9, and 10 into three rows of three (one row on top of the other), according to the following clues:

- There are at least two of each number.
- Each 9 borders an 8 and a 10, either horizontally or vertically.
- Each 8 borders a 10 and a 7, either horizontally or vertically.

We've provided one of the 9s to get you started.

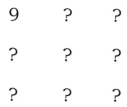

9	?	?
?	?	?
?	?	?

More than half of all doctors in Finland are female.

241. "HONE" IN ON IT

The answer to each clue below includes the word "hone." It might be at the beginning, the end, or in the middle. For example, if the clue were "pioneers sometimes called them Snake Indians, but they called themselves this," the answer would be "Shoshone." What are these three things?

1. One thing you might call a liar.

2. Originally known as a "speaking trumpet."

3. The study of sounds and speech.

242. IDIOMATIC IDIOSYNCRASIES

In this puzzle, the set of letters below represents the words of a popular English idiom. If CBARAAHP stands for "Caught between a rock and a hard place," what other well-known idiom do the following letters stand for? And what is the missing letter?

D_AD

243. THE FAIRY FASHION SHOW

All the fairies in Never Never Land had gathered at the town square for the annual May Day fashion show. But three fairies—Green, Blue, and Yellow—were late.

1. The first late fairy to arrive said she was tardy because she'd misplaced her favorite wand and had to spend time looking for it.

2. The Yellow Fairy said she was late because her ladybug roommates had hidden her wings.

3. The fairy who arrived at 3:10 p.m. said she was late because she'd spilled fairy dust all over her living room and the furniture started to levitate.

4. The Blue Fairy was four minutes late and doesn't use fairy dust.

5. The fairy who was 10 minutes late wore magic shoes in the fashion show.

6. The fairy who wore the jeweled crown got to the fashion show eight minutes before one of the others.

7. The fairy who arrived last wore the feathered dress in the show.

At what time did the three late fairies arrive, why was each one was late, and what did each one wear in the fashion show?

---

244. PASS THE BASKET

Bob walked out of his house, put something in a basket, drove into town, and knocked on the door of a friend. He handed his friend the basket, went home, and never saw another sunrise. What did Bob put in the basket?

245. LANGUAGE EQUATION

If "16 = O. in a P." stands for "16 ounces in a pound," what does this equation stand for?

$$2 = H. of C.$$

246. THINK ABOUT IT

What device that we use to tell time has the most moving parts?

247. THE PROVERB CODE

In the two common English proverbs below, we've changed all the letters except "M" and "Y": consonants are represented by the letter "B" and vowels by the letter "E." The punctuation is the same. Can you sort out what the proverbs are?

1. EEBY BEME, EEBY BE.

2. BEB'B BEEBB YEEB BBEBBEBB

BEBEBE BBEY BEBBB.

248. SEQUENTIAL THINKING

What number should come next in this series?

74, 65, 57, 50, 44, ?

249. THIS OR THAT

What word fits both definitions?

"A kind of fish" or "to complain"

250. THREE'S THE KEY

Can you find a way to combine four 3s so that their value equals 34?

251. ECHOES

What two homophones (words that sound alike but are spelled differently) are being described here?

Smelly chicken

252. SHOP 'TIL YOU DROP

One Tuesday, Mrs. Broom had nothing to do, so she decided to clean house. And it's a lucky thing she did, because she found an old stash of $1 bills long forgotten in a closet.

Immediately after seeing the cash, she said, "Oh my, I must go shopping!" So she stuffed the bills in her jacket pocket—which, unknown to her, had a hole in it—and headed out the door.

A single dollar fell from Mrs. Broom's pocket as she entered the Everything You Need department store. She then used half the remaining money to buy an iron. Two more bills escaped her pocket as she headed over to electronics, where she spent half of her remaining money on a radio. Two more dollars floated to the floor.

Then she spent half of what was left for a set of buttons. Finally, two more dollars were lost before she spent half of the rest of the money for a candy bar. Her last, forlorn dollar fell from her pocket as she left the store.

How many dollar bills did Mrs. Broom have when she left home, and how much did she spend for each item?

253. FLIP-FLOPPED

Each of the clues below will lead you to a compound word, whose two halves differ by only one vowel; the consonants are all the same. For example, if the clue were "a beach sandal," the answer would be "flip-flop." What are these three things?

1. A mix of things

2. It precedes "paddy-whack" in a song.

3. "Balderdash!" (or a snack first manufactured in the 1960s)

254. TO BE OR NOT TO B

What's wrong with these four words?

> Resid
>
> Skat
>
> Revers
>
> Employe

255. DOUBLE TROUBLE

Three couples, including the Murphys, were called down to the police station as witnesses to a crime. In each pair, one person always tells the truth, but the other always lies. Use the clues below to help the cops figure out who lies and who tells the truth.

1. Ben said his wife was a liar. His wife, who is not Britney, said her name was Jennifer.

2. The female in the Webb pair told Allen that her husband's name was Dan.

3. The male in the Carroll pair and Kelly both have a spouse who is a liar.

256. WORD MASH

Hidden in the five words below is an eight-letter word for "someone with petty objections." What you need to do is determine which letters are extraneous and then puzzle out the right word. The answer's letters appear in the right order in the five clue words, and none of the necessary letters are repeated...unless they appear twice in the mystery word. What's the hidden word?

AQUA ION BAN ABLE RAID

Bird with the longest wingspan: the Andean condor, at 10.5 feet.

257. AROUND THE WORLD

The current and former capital of this country are anagrams of each other. What are the cities and the country?

258. WEDDING PARTY

Three bridesmaids from Logic Lovers Lane were headed to a wedding reception. Their husbands arrived to pick them up, and each man carried a bouquet of flowers.

1. Lauren's date was not the man with the roses.

2. Zac brought lilies.

3. The man with the sunflowers did not take Allison to the reception.

4. Brian's wife was named Morgan.

5. James brought roses.

Who was each woman's date to the reception, and what kind of flowers did he bring?

259. TEASER

Two soccer teams met for a game. The Raiders scored five goals but were beaten by the Pirates, who scored six times. Curiously, the Pirates managed to win without a single man kicking the ball. How did they do it?

260. WILD & WOOLLY WORDY

Can you figure out what word or phrase this stands for?

But

Thought   Thought

261. NAME GAME

Can you think of a man's first name that can be transformed into six different women's names just by changing the vowel sound?

262. A PARTY FOR THE AGES

Ralph and Rebecca threw a birthday barbeque for their son. They invited seven neighborhood kids to the party but couldn't remember how old any of them were. (Ralph and Rebecca needed the information to know what party favors to buy.) Here's what they did remember:

1. Audrey was twice as old as Max, and Josie was half of Gabi's age.

2. Two years ago, Danny was the same age that Vicki is now. Today, he's twice as old as Audrey was 10 years ago and three times as old as Josie.

3. Daisy was the "oldest" of the set of triplets who attended.

4. Danny was younger than Audrey.

5. How old was each neighborhood kid?

263. RIDDLER

I am a common English word, five letters long. I don't need to be capitalized, and I include both a silent P and a silent S. What word am I?

264. WILD RIDE

On the reality TV show *Wilderness Gone Wild!*, contestants are taught a survival skill and then left in the jungle with nothing but one luxury item, one of which was a book of brainteasers. The person who comes out of the jungle first wins the competition. This season's show had four contestants, one of whom was named Lucy. Using the clues below, assign each person the correct survival skill and luxury item, and determine in what order they all walked out of the jungle.

1. Jake left the jungle just before the person who gathered fruit and just after the person whose luxury item was lipstick.

2. Both the fire maker and Rob came out of the jungle before the person who carried shampoo.

3. The contestant who was the swimmer came out of the jungle just before the one who carried shaving cream.

4. One of the survival skills was tree climbing.

5. Jen emerged from the jungle sometime after Rob, but she didn't come in last.

6. Jake carried shampoo.

265. IN YOUR ESTIMATION...

How many penny thicknesses are there in a penny's diameter?

266. THE CASE OF THE MISSING LETTERS

The groups of letters below are parts of larger words, but something's missing: the first two and last two letters. What's more, the missing letters are the same: for example, if the given letters were QUI, the missing letters would be "RE"...to form the word REQUIRE. See if you can figure out what these larger words should be.

1. AMMA

2. GIB

267. WORD MATH

If FRONT + BACK = 8, then what does MIGHTY + MOUSE equal?

268. GROWING DOWN

Changing one letter at a time, can you go from MAN to BOY in three steps?

269. THE NAME'S THE GAME

Five old college buddies were such good friends that after graduation they decided to name their motor vehicles after each other. None of the vehicles had the same names as their owners, and no pair of guys named their vehicles after each other.

1. Brad drove a pickup truck.

2. Michael rode a motorcycle.

3. Aaron zipped around town in a Porsche.

4. Dan drove a dune buggy.

5. The motorcycle was named Ben.

6. The pickup truck was named Dan.

7. The VW van's name was the same as the guy whose vehicle was named Brad.

8. Ben's brother's vehicle was named Michael.

What vehicle belonged to Ben's brother?

Yams are more closely related to lilies than they are to sweet potatoes.

270. A CIRCUITOUS ROUTE

We've hidden six six-letter words in the puzzle below. Starting at 1 and moving around the circle, choose one letter from each of the numbered sections to form a common English word. The letters will appear in the same order as the sections, and each letter in a section is used only once. Can you put all six words together?

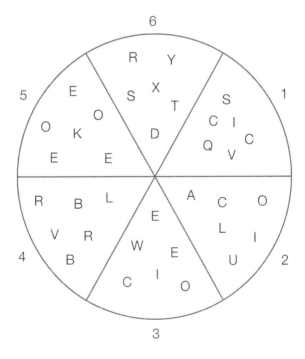

10 percent of all protein consumed by humans worldwide is insects.

271. INSPECTOR LOO INVESTIGATES A MURDER ON THE HIGH SEAS

Gumshoe Commodius Loo strolled the deck of an old galleon-turned-passenger ship called the *Floating Beluga*. Just as a hint of sea spray skimmed his cheek, the ship's porter appeared—wide-eyed and panting—at Loo's side. "Come quickly," he huffed. "There's been a murder!"

Loo followed the young man to the captain's office, where he met the second-in-command, Joe Thornton.

"I'm so glad you're here," Thornton said. "Alastair Reagan texted me and said he caught a blond woman sneaking around the captain's office. By the time I got here, she was gone and Alastair was dead!"

Indeed, the security guard named Reagan lay in a pool of blood on the office floor. There was a gun in his right hand, a set of office keys clenched in his left fist, and an empty holster strapped to his left hip. Across the room, Loo found a desk drawer that looked like it had been pried open.

"The cash box is missing," the porter wailed. "I should have moved that to the safe last night. There was $5,000 in it!" The porter retreated to a corner, sure that he'd be fired and kicked off the ship at the next stop.

Loo turned to face the porter and Thornton. He said, "This was definitely an inside job...and one of you knows it." How did the good inspector figure that out?

There are 200,000 Mary Kay salespeople in China.

272. WHAT'S UP, TEACH?

Monty English taught math at the local high school. Sometimes, though, he forgot to take home his students' homework papers to grade, so he had to make an extra trip back to the school to pick them up.

Yesterday evening, while Monty was driving home from work, his wife sent him a text message reminding him to bring the homework.

After muttering "Aha!" to himself, he turned the car around, headed back to school, got the homework, and then went home. When he got there, he told his wife that her message had saved him an hour of driving. "If you hadn't sent it," he said, "I'd have driven twice as much as usual tonight."

How long had Monty been driving when he got his wife's text?

273. RIDDLER

I'm so fragile that just saying my name breaks me. What am I?

274. QUICK TRICK

Use all of these numbers (1, 2, 3, 4, 5, 6, 9) in any combination, but only one time each, to make the following equation work:

$$? - ? \times ? = ?$$

275. SAM LOYD CLASSIC: RIDING AGAINST THE WIND

See if you can solve this classic by puzzle-maker extraordinaire Sam Loyd (1841–1911): A bicycle rider went a mile in three minutes with the wind, and returned in four minutes against the wind. How long would it take him to bike a mile if there were no wind?

The average adult woman weighs about as much as 134 average rats.

276. SCIENCE SUPERSTARS

Whiz Kids Elementary School held its annual science fair last week, and four students were awarded medals.

1. The student who made a comet didn't place fourth, and Max didn't place third.

2. The student who grew mold placed higher than Brendan.

3. The student who built the talking robot came in first.

4. The student who grew mold placed higher than the one who made the comet.

5. Melissa's project tested whether or not classical music helped plants grow faster.

6. Alison did not grow mold.

In what order did the students place, and who did which project?

277. ANAGRAMMIT

An anagram is a word or phrase that is formed by re-arranging the letters of another word or phrase. For example, "MEAT" can be rearranged to get "TAME" or "MATE." What common 10-letter words can you make with these anagrams?

A TINIEST OH

AVERTED SUN

A TART NURSE

278. FRATERNAL TRIPLETS

To complete this puzzle, fill in the blanks with three words that differ by only one letter. The letter will be in the same position in all three words. Here's an example: The students had to _____ carefully to see when the new _____ of chicks would _____. Add "watch," "batch," and "hatch."

The hedge ____ at London's Hampton Court Palace made so many twists and turns that it sent Tiffany into a stunned ____, and all she could do was ____ in awe.

279. A LEAF FROM THE FAMILY TREE

Lea has no brothers or sisters, so what's her relationship to Janet if Janet's grandmother is Lea's father's daughter?

280. THE BOSS'S BIG IDEA

Bert owned an air-transport company that had only two planes and two pilots, both of whom were hotshots and considered the planes to be their own. This dismayed Bert, who wanted to fire them for flying recklessly, but always gave in because good pilots were hard to find.

One day, Bert thought of a brilliant way to encourage the pilots to be careful. He told them that he would give the one whose plane came in last in a 100-mile race a day off with double pay.

Come race day, the two planes took off on Bert's signal. Did they fly low and slow, each vying for second place? Of course not. They zoomed by at tremendous speed and finished the race in record time. But if the men wanted the extra money and day off, why did they try to beat each other?

Studies show: Dogs with sharp, pointy faces live longer than dogs with flat faces.

281. REUNITED

Six college buddies—with the last names of Smith, Jones, Garcia, Romanov, Grant, and Walsh; and the first names of Katie, Trisha, Jamie, Eddie, Dana, and Jack—all met up at a rock concert for an unofficial reunion. Before the show, the six compared their tickets to see who was sitting next to whom.

1. Katie sat somewhere to the left of Smith, to the right of Walsh, and to the right of Trisha.

2. Jamie sat to the left of at least three of his old friends, including Garcia and Romanov.

3. Dana sat just to the right of Jack and just to the left of Smith.

4. Three friends sat between Jones and Walsh, and one sat between Garcia and Romanov.

5. Romanov's first name was not Jack.

What are the first and last names of each person, and in what order (from left to right) did they sit at the concert?

282. WILD & WOOLLY WORDY

Can you figure out what word
or phrase this stands for?

```
M M E A L M
E         E
A         A
L M E A L L
```

283. MORE THAN ONE WAY TO SKIN A CAT

A mischievous linguistics professor wrote a familiar six-word proverb on the blackboard. The first and fourth words were both "out." He then asked the class if it were possible to restate the old saw in two words. A creative young woman raised her hand and said, "Blind maniac."

What was the proverb?

284. PREFERENCES

Aunt Abby is off to the jewelry store to buy herself a birthday present. She loves opals, but dislikes diamonds. Given that she also prefers the following—deans over professors, nobles over lords, and hibiscuses over hydrangeas—can you deduce what criteria Aunt Abby uses to choose her favorite things?

285. IT'S ALL ELEMENTAL

We've hidden nine elements from the periodic table in the grid below. You can find each word by connecting a series of squares diagonally, horizontally, or vertically. For example, "gold" can be found by starting with the letter G in the bottom right corner, moving up one space to the O, down diagonally to L, and horizontally left to D. Not all the letters will be used. See if you can find the other eight elements.

B	Z	R	O	F
I	O	X	N	E
C	N	Y	G	N
A	G	O	P	I
B	R	M	T	O
I	U	D	L	G

286. BIRTHDAY BONUS

The day before yesterday, Alex was 17. Next year, he'll be 20. When is Alex's birthday?

287. TEASER

Luke ordered a cup of coffee at a restaurant and, just as he went to take a drink, noticed a piece of plastic floating in it. "Waiter!" He shouted. "There's some plastic in my coffee. Please bring me a fresh cup." The waiter apologized profusely, took the cup, and brought Luke a second cup of coffee. The plastic was gone, but when Luke took a drink, he knew immediately that the waiter hadn't poured him a fresh cup. How did he know?

288. BACKWORDS

Read from right to left—there are two five-letter words hidden backward in the line of letters below. Do you see them?

S T O A T R I K S W E A D T H G U O G R

289. FRATERNAL TRIPLETS

To complete this puzzle, fill in the blanks with three words that differ by only one letter. The letter will be in the same position in all three words. Here's an example: The students had to _____ carefully to see when the new _____ of chicks would _____. Add "watch," "batch," and "hatch."

The kindhearted ornithologist, observing that winter was just ____, worried that food would be scarce and her favorite ____ would be ____ by spring.

290. A NUMBERS GAME

All of the numbers in the problem below (except the second and third numbers in the answer) have been replaced by letters. Can you figure out what numbers each letter represents so that the math is correct?

$$
\begin{array}{r}
M\,M\,E \\
\times\ M\,M\,E \\
\hline
E\,0{,}6\,M\,E
\end{array}
$$

291. INSPECTOR LOO AND THE CRYPTO CLUB

When Inspector Commodius Loo was in college, he wanted to join the Crypto Club, a secret society of budding code-crackers. But getting in wasn't easy. Before each meeting, prospective members had to line up on the quad at midnight while the Supreme Cryptographer—nicknamed "Soup"—gave each person a coded message. The wannabe code breaker then had to decipher the code on the spot and answer in a way that showed he got it.

For months, Loo lurked nearby and listened to the exchanges. Here's some of what he heard: "Who is the current president of the United States?" asked Soup. "Wordsworth," answered the first person in line. He got in. Another time, Soup said, "How are you tonight?" "Hercules!" said the student. She got in too. Soup once greeted a fellow student with, "Say something twice." "Stinkpot!" was the reply. He gained entry as well.

Finally, one night, Loo stepped into the line. "And who might you be?" asked Soup. "Anteater!" shouted Loo, whereupon Soup welcomed the club's newest member. How did Loo know what to say?

292. WILD & WOOLLY WORDY

Can you figure out what word or phrase this stands for?

langforuage

293. WORD MASH

Hidden in the five words below is an eight-letter word for "a nighttime burrower." What you need to do is determine which letters are extraneous and then puzzle out the right word. The answer's letters appear in the right order in the five clue words, and none of the necessary letters are repeated...unless they appear twice in the mystery word. What's the hidden word?

FAN CARD VINE OAR KISS

294. QUICK TRICK

Using all the numbers 1 through 9 in order, come up with an equation that equals 28. (Hint: You may need to combine some of the adjacent numbers.)

295. TRUTH OR LIE?

Twins Adam and Anya take turns lying during the week. On Sundays, Mondays, and Tuesdays, Adam tells lies—he tells the truth on the other days. On Wednesdays, Thursdays, and Fridays, Anya lies, but she tells the truth on all the other days. This morning, they both said, "Tomorrow, I'll lie." What day of the week is it, and which twin is telling the truth?

296. THIS WAS NO PICNIC

Three time travelers stumbled into a desert village in ancient Mesopotamia but soon discovered that only two of them had brought any water. The third traveler (who was getting increasingly thirsty) suggested that they share the water, and he'd pay the other two the value of what he drank. His comrades agreed.

The first man pulled out five bottles of water from his rucksack; the second man produced three bottles, all of which they shared equally. Afterward, the third man offered up eight bronze coins to pay for his portion. The others thought that was sufficient, but then they started fighting over how to divide up the money. A wise camel trader decided the matter fairly. How did he do it?

Ricky Nelson's "Travelin' Man" (1961) was offered to and rejected by Sam Cooke.

297. MATHEMATICAL MADNESS

Use the numbers 1 through 9 to fill in the empty spots below. Each number is used only once.

	+		x		=	40
+		x		x		
	+		+		=	18
x		-		+		
	-		x		=	21
=		=		=		
35		34		31		

Artist Paul Klee signed his paintings with a clover symbol...

298. RAPID FIRE

• You can take away my whole and still have some left. You can take away some and still have my whole left. What am I?

• When Dana first learned to drive, she went up a one-way street the wrong way but didn't break the law. How?

299. SEQUENTIAL THINKING

What number comes next in this series?

1 2 4 14 21 ?

300. QUOTE ME

Rearrange the anagram in the brackets to figure out what Bill Cosby was trying to say.

"[TO LIMIT ARMY] is a long shot, I admit. But somebody has to be first."

—**Bill Cosby**

...Klee is German for "clover."

301. SUNDAY DRIVE

Bernie Welloff owned five classic cars: a Bentley, a Jaguar, a Porsche, a Ferrari, and a Mercedes. Every Sunday afternoon, he took one of them out for a spin with one of his five best friends: Skip, Arty, Dude, Leo, and Jack. This particular Sunday, Bernie's cook wanted to order in a nice dinner for her boss and his friend, but to know what to order, she needed to figure out which friend Bernie was with (she had a list of all their favorite foods). Here's what she knew.

1. Bernie never drove in the same car or with the same friend two Sundays in a row.

2. Skip was in the Bahamas.

3. Bernie never drove the Jaguar in the rain.

4. Leo rode only in the Mercedes.

5. Last week, Bernie and Dude drove in the Bentley.

6. On Friday, weathermen had predicted wet weather for the weekend.

7. The Mercedes had an oil leak.

8. Bernie had stopped driving the Ferrari because its bright purple interior clashed with his clothes.

9. Arty never rode in the Porsche.

10. Bernie didn't drive any of the cars if they had mechanical problems.

After giving it some thought, the cook put in the dinner order. Who was staying for the meal, and what car was Bernie driving that Sunday?

302. NO PARK-ING

Two friends keep missing each other at the park. Ben stops by at 4:00 p.m. every 13 days, hoping to see his old friend Aaron, who goes to the park at 4:00 p.m. every 17 days. If the friends just missed each other when Ben stopped by on New Year's Eve and Aaron came on New Year's Day, when will they actually meet?

303. BICYCLE BOON OR BUST?

Bonnie bought a used bicycle for $40, fixed it up, and sold it to Brian for $50. After talking with some friends, though, she realized she should have asked for more. So she bought the bike back for $60 and then sold it to Jake for $70. In the end, did she come out ahead, lose money, or break even?

China is the most populous country, but 71 other nations are more crowded.

304. INSPECTOR LOO AND THE CASE OF THE SILK STOCKINGS

Detective Commodius Loo was browsing the antique pistols at a flea market when he heard a ruckus from a booth across the way. It turned out that the hosier who owned the booth was missing a pair of silk stockings, and he'd accused three patrons of the crime. Loo sauntered over just as the shopkeeper was about to call the police. "Can I help?" offered the inspector.

"One of those men stole my stockings," complained the shopkeeper, while pointing at the offenders. "They all own different colored coats, but they set the coats down and now refuse to pick them up. I'll tell you this: men with blue coats always lie, men with white coats sometimes lie, and men with red coats always

tell the truth. So if you figure out who owns what coat, we can catch the dirty rotten thief."

The first suspect said nothing, but the shopkeeper whispered to Loo, "The first guy said he hadn't stolen the stockings and that he owned a red coat...or a white coat. I forget exactly."

The second suspect pointed at the first and declared, "Whatever that guy says is a lie."

The third suspect smirked, "The first guy was wearing a blue coat when I walked over here."

That was all the good inspector needed to know. He raised a bushy eyebrow and announced that he'd fingered the culprit. Who was it?

The band playing the "cantina" scene in *Star Wars*...

305. TRICKY, TRICKY

Laurel was stuck in freeway traffic behind a Volkswagen hatchback with the following vanity license plate: ML8 ML8. What color was that car?

306. CELESTIAL WORDPLAY

Changing one letter at a time, can you go from STAR to MOON in six steps?

307. LOOKING FOR LINCOLN

Andy offered Thom the following bet: "I'm going to drop this $5 bill, and I bet you $10 that it will land with Abraham Lincoln faceup. If it doesn't, I'll give you $15." Should Thom take the bet?

...is called Figrin D'an and the Modal Nodes.

308. BACKTRACKING

By reading backward, you can find at least seven common four-letter words in the given words. No fair changing the order of the letters, but you are allowed to skip over letters. Here's an example: in the word TENDER, you'll find RENT, but not REND. How many words can you identify?

> **1.** EXTREMITIES
> **2.** MAGNETICALLY

309. CONNECTIONS

The following words have something in common. What is it?

> MEAN, STUPID, ALLERGIC, TIRED,
> TIMID, HEALING, CONTENT

310. ECHOES

What two homophones (words that sound alike but are spelled differently) are being described here?

Run away from a bug

311. FILL 'ER UP

Let's say you've got two glasses: one holds four ounces of liquid, and the other holds nine ounces. But you need to measure out six ounces of root beer for your daughter. How would you measure out the soda to make sure she gets the right amount?

The average American will spend $20,000 on fast food in a lifetime.

312. IDIOMATIC IDIOSYNCRASIES

In this puzzle, the set of letters below represents the words of a popular English idiom. If CBARAAHP stands for "Caught between a rock and a hard place," what other well-known idiom do the following letters stand for? And what is the missing letter?

TEBC_W

313. A NUMBERS GAME

This math problem needs some numbers. Can you figure out what number each letter stands for and puzzle out the right answer?

$$
\begin{array}{r}
ED \\
\times\ ED \\
\hline
TVA \\
DGV \\
\hline
DIVA \\
\end{array}
$$

314. TRICKY, TRICKY

Can you figure out the rule we've used to arrange the numbers below?

$$
\begin{array}{ccc}
5 & 4 & 9 \\
1 & 6 & 2 \\
8 & 7 & 3 \\
\end{array}
$$

There's enough sulfur in your body to kill all the fleas on a single dog.

315. THE CASE OF THE MISSING LETTERS

The groups of letters below are parts of larger words, but something's missing: the first two and last two letters. What's more, the missing letters are the same: for example, if the given letters were QUI, the missing letters would be RE...to form the word REQUIRE. See if you can figure out what these larger words should be. (Hint: Proper nouns are allowed.)

1. ARDU

2. DE

316. THE PROVERB CODE

In the two common English proverbs below, we've changed all the letters except N and Y: consonants are represented by the letter B and vowels by the letter E. The punctuation is the same. What are the proverbs?

1. E BEN BBE EB BEB EBN BEBYEB BEB E

BEEB BEB E BBEENB.

2. E BEBEN'B BEBB EB BEBEB BENE.

317. THE CANTERBURY COOK-OFF

The town of Canterbury, Connecticut, holds a cook-off every year. This year, bakers competed in two categories: cakes and cookies. In the cakes competition, Jonathan came in second, the 20-year-old won, Anna placed ahead of the 23-year-old, and the 24-year-old was third. In the cookie competition, Jonathan placed ahead of Lisa, Anna came in third, and the 21-year old won. The person who placed last in cookies was third in cakes, and only one person finished in the same position in both competitions. Also, Sean is three years younger than Lisa.

What is each baker's age and where did each place in the two competitions?

318. AROUND THE WORD

In the wheel below, start with the letter B and work your way clockwise back to B, identifying common English words as you go. Each word must include at least three letters. The letters will overlap, and many words are nested in others. Don't skip any letters—they'll all be used at least once.

How many can you find?

Americans are more likely to recycle than to vote.

319. BACKWORDS

Reading from right to left, there are two five-letter words hidden backward in the line of letters below. Do you see them?

V C T I W A F I G H T R A E Y L E V E R

320. TREED

Some people are just naturally good at clambering around the old family tree and figuring out the complex relationships among individuals. (Others are content with sitting around the trunk drinking lemonade.) Which group are you in? Can you figure out what relation to you these family members would be?

1. Your brother's wife's husband's grandfather's wife

2. Your sister's father's stepson's mother

321. CAN YOU UNMAKE THIS MESS?

It was almost naptime at the Tiny Tots Day-Care Center, which also meant that it was clean-up time. The kids had been playing with two kinds of toys that morning: blocks and dolls. Three Tiny Tots—Joey, Emma, and Bryce—were in charge of putting everything away.

After a little hemming and hawing, the kids got to work, and when they were finished, their teachers counted up what toys the kids had collected to put away. Joey had three times as many dolls as Emma, who had four times as many blocks as Bryce.

Each child had picked up exactly the same number of toys, and as a group, they'd gathered the same number of dolls and blocks. In all, the three kids had picked up fewer than 200 toys.

How many dolls and blocks were collected in all, and how many did each child pick up?

322. RIDDLER

I have no wheels, yet can still be driven. You slice me, but I remain whole. What am I?

323. DIRTY DOGS

This year's Down and Dirty Dog Show had whittled its competitors down to Bubba and two other top dogs, who went snout-to-snout in the last round: the talent competition. Based on the clues below, determine where each dog placed and what his talent was.

1. The winning dog was named Sparkles.

2. One of the dogs herded mechanical squirrels.

3. Meathead came in last and did not play Frisbee catch.

4. The dog that juggled water bowls came in second.

324. A NUMBERS GAME

This math problem needs some numbers. Can you figure out what number each letter stands for and puzzle out the right answer?

$$
\begin{array}{r}
UG \\
\times\ UG \\
\hline
TUG \\
GO\ \ \\
\hline
BUG
\end{array}
$$

325. PREFERENCES

Olivia likes Monopoly better than Scrabble, oranges better than grapes, and tango over swing. Oh, and she thinks *Twilight* is a substandard film, but *High Noon* is high art. Do you think her favorite animal is a kangaroo or a kiwi?

326. SAY "UNCLE!"

The arm-wrestling tournament at Barney's Bar and Grille was in full swing. After a rousing final round, the restaurant crowned a winner. The finalists were Cisco, Abe, Hank, and Chris. From the clues below, can you figure out the order in which each man finished?

1. Chris ranked lower than Hank.

2. Cisco and Abe majored in zoology at the same college.

3. The man who came in third said to the winner, "It's so great to meet you. I've heard stories about your legendary barbeque skills."

4. Cisco was still the object of many jokes because, at Chris's daughter's christening a few years back, he spilled an entire bowl of black beans down the front of his white dress shirt.

5. The competitor who came in second had dropped out of school in the 10th grade and had never gotten married.

327. RAPID FIRE

• Its "thunder" comes before lightning, its "lightning" comes before clouds, and its "rain" dries everything out. What is it?

• Using only addition and the number 9 nine times, create an equation that totals 1,215.

328. DYNAMIC TRIOS

We've removed all the consonants (including Ys) from the pairs of words below, but the pairs have something in common. Can you deduce what the common thread is, and what consonants are missing? To help you out, we put the list in alphabetical order.

    1. _ E _ _ & E _ _ I E

    2. _ A _ E _ _ E & _ _ I _ _ E _

    3. _ A _ _ _ A _ O _ & _ E _ A _ _ _ E _ _

329. THE INHERITANCE

Mr. Thistlebottom was an old codger with four heirs. He also liked number games. When he died, Thistlebottom bequeathed his money as follows, and the heirs had to figure out the amounts:

1. To Arlen, twice as much as to Linda.

2. To Jackie, twice as much as to Arlen.

3. To Stan, twice as much as to Jackie.

If Mr. Thistlebottom's estate was valued at $150,000, how much money did each person get?

330. BACKWORDS

Reading from right to left, there are two five-letter words hidden backward in the line of letters below. Do you see them?

C H C T I W N N O I N O S E N S E T H O

331. A PUZZLING TRIP

A bus full of people was traveling over a bridge on its way to Las Vegas. No one got on or off the bus, but when it reached the other side, there wasn't a single person onboard. How is that possible?

332. LETTER PLAY

Each group of letters below is a complete set. Can you figure out what each grouping represents? For example, if the given letters were "A, E, I, O, U," the answer would be "vowels." (Hint: We've alphabetized the lists.)

1. B C N M V X Z
2. A B O

333. TRICKY, TRICKY

Study this paragraph. What's odd about it? Look at its words. If lucky, you will find out what's so unusual about it. Do you know what it is now? Look again. Don't miss anything. It actually isn't too hard.

334. PUT ME IN, COACH!

Vinnie, Ronnie, and Matt were all proud dads with sons who were named after them: Vinnie Jr., Ronnie Jr., and Matt Jr. All of the boys played on the same Little League baseball team. One was the shortstop, one pitched, and the other played center field. Here's what we know:

1. The center fielder often played basketball with his dad.

2. Vinnie Jr. didn't like the shortstop.

3. Every Tuesday, the shortstop's dad went golfing with his wife.

4. Ronnie never played games or sports.

Who played center field?

335. CONNECTIONS

The five words listed here have something in common. What is it?

SHORE

TOGA

EMANATE

RAPTOR

SANDIER

336. WHAT'S HIS LINE OF WORK?

Max, Bert, and Cameron were remarkable men: each had not just one but two occupations that he enjoyed equally. The jobs were gambler, bricklayer, bartender, pool hustler, physician, and street musician. Now it's your occupation to deduce from the given facts what two jobs each man held.

1. The gambler offended the bartender by laughing at the way he poured draft.

2. Both the bartender and the physician used to play air hockey with Max.

3. The pool hustler got some advice on building a wall from the bricklayer.

4. The gambler was sweet on the pool hustler's sister.

5. Bert owed the physician $175.

6. Cameron beat both Bert and the pool hustler at darts every time they played together.

337. LANGUAGE EQUATION

If "16 = O. in a P." stands for "16 ounces in a pound," what does this equation stand for?

10 = D. in a D.

338. WORD SCRAMBLE

We've broken apart and hidden six words in the grid below: one is a general topic, and the other five relate to it. Each square is used only once. Can you put the letters back together to decipher the scrambled words?

D	BU	DO	ER	O
BO	OO	ND	I	BL
O	L	X	OU	L
G	GS	E	LL	DH
OO	C	LE	P	D

339. WORD MYSTERY

Use the clues to figure out the mysterious word.

1. I am eight letters long.

2. My last four letters spell something that babies have more of than adults.

3. Letters 2, 3, 5, and 8 spell something to relax in.

4. Using just letters 4 and 8, I'm you.

5. Put all my letters together, and I'm a musical instrument.

What am I?

340. KOUNTING KIDS

There are three kids in the Kantor family: a set of twins and a younger child. All are less than 10 years old, so if you write down their ages from the youngest to the oldest, you'll get a three-digit number. The children's mother, Mrs. Kantor, is not a teenager, and her age can be divided into that three-digit number exactly. Furthermore, the result of dividing Mrs. Kantor's age into the three-digit number is the sum of the children's three ages. So how old are Mrs. Kantor and her three kids?

The Dead Sea is six times as salty as the Atlantic Ocean.

341. INSPECTOR LOO AND THE CASE OF THE MURDERED MATRON

Inspector Commodius Loo took a puff of his cigar and surveyed the scene before him: Tamara McCann, wife of über-lawyer to the stars Andrew McCann, lay dead on the living-room floor of the couple's New York City penthouse.

"It was definitely homicide," said the detective working the case. The living room was a mess—lamps were broken, books strewn about. And the kitchen wasn't much better. Dishes lay in pieces, and it looked like Tamara had been baking before she was killed: a dozen cupcakes sat on a plate on the counter, half of them frosted neatly with the buttercream in the bowl next to them.

"When did you leave for work this morning?" Loo asked Andrew McCann, who sat weeping on the sofa.

"About seven, but I came back for lunch," McCann said. "Tamara and I had sandwiches, and then she said she was going to frost those cupcakes for the country club bake sale. I got home a few hours later and saw this!"

"What did you do when you got home?" asked Loo.

"I checked on Tamara first, of course, and then I called 911. Then I turned on the air conditioner. It was hot as Hades in here." (The city was having a summer heatwave.)

Loo flashed a knowing smile, took another puff off his cigar, and then told the detective to arrest Andrew McCann. How did he know Tamara's husband had committed the crime?

1 in 5,000 North Atlantic lobsters is born bright blue.

342. CURIOUS CONNECTIONS

It's not obvious, but these words have something in common:

CUBA

DRAM

CRUMPET

HARM

MIDDLE

CELLS

Figure out the connection, and then decide which of these words belongs with those above.

MUTUAL

FINE

DANDY

TRENCH

343. ANAGRAMMIT

An anagram is a word or phrase that's formed by rearranging the letters of another word or phrase. For example, "MEAT" can be rearranged to get "TAME" or "MATE." What common 10-letter words can you make with these anagrams?

STATIC PAIL

MONGER VENT

BLAZED BOOM

344. A FUNNY SITUATION

For many years, Zeno was the head of a school for comedians. Someone once asked him how many students he had. Zeno—being mischievous, even for a comic—answered, "Half study stand-up, a quarter slapstick, one-seventh study writing, and there are three others who are so whacked-out that I let them do whatever they want."

How many students attended Zeno's school? (Hint: Find a number that's equal to its half plus its quarter plus its seventh plus three.)

345. SAM LOYD CLASSIC: PUZZLING PRATTLE

See if you can solve this classic by puzzle-maker extraordinaire Sam Loyd (1841–1911): Two children, who were confused about what day of the week it was, stopped by a circus poster to straighten things out. That's when a third child, Priscilla, who was hoping they'd ask her to join them at the show, said to John, "When the day after tomorrow is yesterday, 'today' will be as far from Sunday as that day was which was 'today' when the day before yesterday was 'tomorrow.'"

What day of the week was it?

346. WORDPLAY

In what well-known word do these six consecutive consonants appear?

TCHPHR

347. CASTLE RESTAURANTS

Uncle John's favorite niece, Amy Loo, loves to eat. She also loves anything made of stone. So last summer, she took a trip abroad to visit castles with restaurants. When she got back, she made the following observations:

1. Castles open year-round are on mountaintops.

2. When the food is good, the castle staff is friendly.

3. Castles with stained-glass windows have roses climbing up their walls.

4. The food is bad only in run-down castles.

5. Run-down castles don't allow guests with motorcycles.

6. Castles with unfriendly staff are open for only part of the year.

7. Castles without stained-glass windows aren't on mountaintops.

In the places that Amy Loo visited, can a motorcycling guest enjoy the sight of climbing roses?

348. PIE CUTS

The Thanksgiving feast was over, and it was time for dessert. Uncle Cuthbert decided to play a game with his niece Christine: If she could cut the family's pumpkin pie into eight pieces using only three cuts, he would give her $5.

How did Christine earn her money?

349. AGE HAZE

One year ago, Mrs. Barnes was five times as old as Ben, who is less than 20 years old now. Today, Mrs. Barnes is three times as old as Larissa will be four years from now, and four times as old as Mary Jane was three years ago.

How old are they all?

...It's an homage to John Belushi's character in *Animal House.*

350. FOUR SQUARE

Without overlapping or breaking any of the tooth-picks, move two of them to make four squares that are all the same size.

351. QUICK TRICK

Today, David is 54 years old, and his dad just turned 80. How old was David's dad when he was three times his son's age?

352. CANDY MAGIC

Clem just bought two candy bars: one was cheap chocolate, and the other was fancy European chocolate. He paid $3.40 total, but the fancy one cost $3 more than the cheap one. How much did each chocolate bar cost?

353. FRATERNAL TRIPLETS

To complete this puzzle, fill in the blanks with three words that differ by only one letter. The letter will be in the same position in all three words. Here's an example: The students had to _____ carefully to see when the new _____ of chicks would _____. Add "watch," "batch," and "hatch."

During lunch, the class bully began to ____ one of the younger kids, and things were getting pretty ___ until a teacher rushed over and in a ____ tone told the bully to cut it out pronto.

The various *Star Trek* series have aired 726 episodes.

354. LETTER PERFECT

Fill in the blanks to make this sentence true:

There are ___ E's, ___ O's, and ___ T's in this sentence.

355. SEQUENTIAL THINKING

What number should come next in this series?

32974, 43297, 74329, ?

356. WILD & WOOLLY WORDY

Can you figure out what word or phrase this stands for?

temper₍a₎ture

temper_ature

In 1939, Eleanor Roosevelt received a telegram powered by electric eel currents.

357. POKER PARADOX

It had been a rough night of poker at the community center—especially for Rick, who had lost $4.85. Meanwhile, Jane, Harriet, and Judd had won $2.80, $1.40, and 65 cents respectively.

The problem was that the cash they had didn't easily square with their chips. Rick had only a $5 bill and a dime. Jane had a dollar bill, a 50-cent piece, and a quarter. Harriet had two $2 bills, a 50-cent piece, and a nickel. Judd had a 50-cent piece, a quarter, and a dime.

After some head-scratching, they came up with a solution. Rick settled with Jane quickly and went home. Then Judd, Jane, and Harriet sorted out the remainder of the transaction. At the end, Jane paid Harriet.

How did they do it?

How many countries have the color brown as their flag's main color? None.

358. FIVE-FINGER DISCOUNT

Six wayward friends (Sarah, James, May, Ryan, Ann, and Ellen) went shoplifting one day. They hit up Skymall, a five-story shopping center, where each person went directly to the floor that had the item he or she wanted to steal. Each purloined just one thing—the objects were a doll, a box of sweet-smelling soaps, a power drill, a baseball, a bedspread, and a pair of earrings.

1. All the friends except Sarah entered the elevator together on the first floor.

2. May and the one who stole the baseball got off at the second floor.

3. One person got off on the third floor to lift a box of sweet-smelling soaps.

4. The person who stole the earrings got off at the fourth floor, leaving Ellen all alone to get off at the fifth floor.

5. Dolls are sold on the first floor.

6. Ann was the fourth person to get out of the elevator.

7. The next day, Jane (who received a power drill as a present from one of the friends who got off on the second floor) went back to the mall to look around and ran into a kid returning the baseball one of the others had given to him.

What did each person steal, and from which floor?

---

359. VOWEL PLAY

We thought and thought...and thought, but were able to come up with only one English word that includes five consecutive vowels. What is it?

360. WILD & WOOLLY WORDY

Can you figure out what word or phrase this stands for?

D
R
A
H

Only two-time Academy Award–winning African American actor: Denzel Washington.

361. ONE SIDE OR THE OTHER

Paul stood on one side of the river. His dog, Bo, stood on the other. "Come here, Bo!" Paul shouted. "Come on, boy." There were no bridges or boats, but Bo managed to cross the river without getting wet. How?

362. FRATERNAL TRIPLETS

To complete this puzzle, fill in the blanks with three words that differ by only one letter. The letter will be in the same position in all three words. Here's an example: The students had to _____ carefully to see when the new _____ of chicks would _____. Add "watch," "batch," and "hatch."

The novelist was puffed up with ____ because today, in the ____ of her life, she was going to be awarded a world-famous, million-dollar ____.

New York City residents may keep bees within the city's limits.

363. BOOK BITE

Three *Bathroom Readers* were stacked vertically next to each other on a bookshelf with their spines facing out. The covers of the books each measured $\frac{1}{8}$". The pages of each book measure 2". If a bookworm started eating at page one of the book on the left, and then ate through the books in a straight line until he got to the last page of the book on the right, how many inches of book would the worm have eaten?

364. CHAIN REACTION

Insert a word between the two given words to create two new words. For example, adding GUN between BLOW and POWDER would produce BLOWGUN and GUNPOWDER.

BLACK _____ ROOM

BIRD _____ STORM

365. MATH TRICK

Think of a number between
1 and 50. Write it down (spelled out)
on a piece of paper. Now, count the
letters in that word to get another
number, and write it down (spelled
out). Keep going until you reach a
number that keeps repeating.
What is that number? (It'll
always be the same.)

A dog's sense of smell is about 45 times better than a human's.

SOLUTIONS

1. SCHOOL RULES Yes

2. THE PROVERB CODE
1. A fool and his money are soon parted.
2. A picture is worth a thousand words.

3. WILD & WOOLLY WORDY Bookends

4. ANAGRAMMIT
1. UNIVERSITY, **2.** QUESTIONER, **3.** PUNISHMENT

5. TRIANGULAR REASONING
First swap the 5 and 7 in the second row. Then swap the 7 with the 3 in the bottom left corner. Each side will now add up to 20.

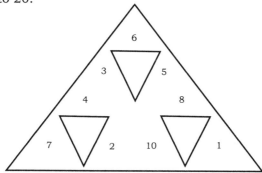

6. FRATERNAL TRIPLETS
topic, toxic, tonic

7. THREE MEN, THREE JOBS
Adam is the butcher, Alex is the baker, and Joe is the candlestick maker. Because Adam is Alex's father-in-law and Adam's wife likes cookies, both men are married. That means Joe is the bachelor and the candlestick maker. If Adam makes more money than the baker, that means he doesn't hold that job, so Adam has to be the butcher. By process of elimination, Alex has to be the baker.

8. LANGUAGE EQUATION
Five fingers on a hand

9. THE SWEET SPOT
$9, for the number of letters in the candy's name.

10. THINK ABOUT IT
If you type the word out in capital letters, it has what's called a "180-degree rotational symmetry," meaning that if the word is turned upside down, it will still spell out SWIMS.

11. ECHOES Bawl ball

12. DIRECTIONS
Here's one way to do it: WEST, PEST, PAST, EAST

13. INSPECTOR LOO AND THE CASE OF THE MISSING BEER STEIN
The beer stein is in the cherry box, opened with the #3 key. The #1 key opens the oak box, the #2 key opens the elm box, and the #4 key opens the maple box. And as for Dollface, Loo let her wait. He doesn't like ultimatums.

14. SAM LOYD CLASSIC: THE PLAYERS WHO ALL WON
The "winning" players were musicians in a band. Loyd never said they were card players.

15. A DAY AT THE RACES
From first to last: the June bug, centipede, butterfly, and snail.

16. QUOTE ME ANGEL MOTHER

17. NESTED WORDS

BIT in AMBITION

18. SUM FUN!

5 + 3 + 9 + 1 + 8 + 6 = 32

19. CROSS CONFUSION

To solve this puzzle, you need to figure out the five-letter opposite for the given word and then put it into the grid:

L	A	U	G	H
S	M	A	R	T
C	L	O	S	E
A	V	O	I	D
B	R	I	E	F

20. RAISING A BET

Hadley lost the bet. Water won't ever cover the three rungs because the yacht and the ladder rise with the tide.

21. IDIOMATIC IDIOSYNCRASIES

The missing letter is T. The idiom is "Rob Peter to pay Paul."

22. BEAUTY'S IN THE EYE OF THE BE-OLDER 61

23. CHAIN REACTION
GREEN back BONE
SAND bar TENDER

24. WHAT'S COOKING?
Turn on switch #1 for a minute or two, and then turn it off. Turn on switch #2 and go into the kitchen. The burner that's warm is controlled by switch #1. The one that's on goes with #2. And the one that's off is controlled by switch #3.

25. IT'S SYMBOLIC

```
      1
     14
    115
+  415
  -----
    545
```

26. WORDPLAY
SNOWING, SOWING, SWING, SING, SIN, IN, I
or SNOWING, SOWING, OWING, WING, WIN, IN, I

27. HERE FISHY, FISHY

Jennifer turned on the hose and filled up the pipe. Mista floated to the top.

28. MIRROR, MIRROR

KAYAK

MADAM or MINIM

TENET

29. LINEAR LOGIC

Move the middle line of the E to between the first two I's to create the word "chip."

30. ANAGRAMMED OPPOSITES

SUNNY/CLOUDY

31. BACKWORDS   FLOAT, UPPER

32. A LITTLE NUMBERS LOGIC

Amy has number 8. The numbers are consecutive, so if

Porter has 9, the only possibilities are 8 and 10. Since the numbers only went up to 10, if Amy had that one, she'd have known by deduction that Porter had to be holding number 9.

33. SPELLING STATES

The letters are N and A. The states that don't use them are Mississippi, Ohio, and Missouri.

34. THE SECRET WORD

SPADE

35. WILD & WOOLLY WORDY

Growing pains

36. BACKTRACKING

1. REEL, REEF, RISE, SELF
2. SLIT, SLAT, SIRE, SINE, SATE, SANE, LIAR, LINE, LATE, LANE

37. HAZY DAYS Saturday

38. DOG SHOWDOWN

8 people and 14 dogs

39. INSPECTOR LOO MEETS A TUCKERED-OUT EXPLORER

The explorer really needed only two Sherpas. The three of them left on the first morning, each carrying four days' worth of food, for a total of 12 days of food. At the end of that day, they all had three days' worth left. The explorer sent the first Sherpa back with one days' worth of food, leaving four days' worth for himself and the remaining Sherpa (a total of eight days' worth). The next morning, the pair traveled for another day, and in the evening, the explorer sent the second Sherpa back with two days' worth of food. That left the explorer a four-day supply for the remaining four days of his climb.

40. FRATERNAL TRIPLETS

fooled, foiled, foaled

41. MISSING NUMBERS

2718 + 3456 = 6174

42. WORD FIND

Affair

43. TREED

1. First cousin

2. Stepmother

3. Brother-in-law

44. SCHOOL DAZE

The answer is 10. Of the 100 kids, 15 of them are not dropped off by their parents, 30 don't carry stuffed animals, 25 don't like cheese sandwiches for lunch, and 20 love apple juice. That makes 90 kids; they could all be different children. That means that the least number who can embody all four characteristics is the remaining 10.

45. EVERYTHING'S COMING UP RICHES

Daisy has three children: George, Joe, and Alicia.

Jennifer has two: Adam and Tom.

Diane has one: Emily.

46. WORD PYRAMID

The words are PACK, PACE, PAGE, PIGS, PITS, and PITH.

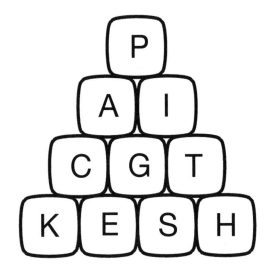

47. ECHOES

Aid (the) aide

48. LANGUAGE EQUATION

12 Days of Christmas

49. THIS OR THAT?

Knot

50. BUGGY

Here's one way to do it: MOTH, MOTE, MITE, MIRE, FIRE

51. QUICK TRICK

He'd make more money selling to two people than to one.

52. NOTABLE QUOTABLE

"Biographies are but the clothes and buttons of the man. The biography of the man himself cannot be written."

53. FOREIGN EXCHANGE

Sophie Chavez arrived from Spain on Friday.

Samantha Garcia arrived from Canada on Saturday.

Lisa Smith arrived from France on Saturday.

Jane Pierre arrived from Mexico on Sunday.

Rachel Jones arrived from Poland on Sunday.

54. DYNAMIC TRIOS

Common food pairings: **1.** COOKIES & MILK
2. HAM & CHEESE **3.** PEANUT BUTTER & JELLY

55. ROAD TRIP

This one is tricky—the reason has to do with the curvature of the Earth and the fact that the distance around the planet is greatest at the equator. The two trips began on the equator. But each family traveled slightly farther on the legs of their trip that run parallel to the equator, making their end points a few miles away from their starting points.

56. WORD MYSTERY

Carpenter

57. WILD & WOOLLY WORDY

Beginning of the end

58. MIX-UP AT THE VET

Mrs. King owns Badger, Mrs. Badger owns Buck, Mrs. Buck owns Boomer, and Mrs. Boomer owns King.

59. MIXED MESSAGE

We found six: ESPRIT, PRIEST, RIPEST, SPRITE, STRIPE, TRIPES

60. ECHOES
Friar fryer

61. BACKWORDS
ALBUM, BRASH

62. SEQUENTIAL THINKING
T and D—the first letters from the words in this series of musical tones: Do, Re, Mi, Fa, So, La, Ti, Do.

63. MYSTERY NUMBER
16

64. INSPECTOR LOO AND THE STOLEN SUMMER
Chris Clever worked on 10 cases, Guy Spy 6, Sherry Sherlock 5, Lucy Loo 4, Dan Detective 3, and Michael Mastermind 2.

65. QUICK TRICK
MAPLE, ELM, SPRUCE

66. IN TWO STRAIGHT LINES...

From tallest to shortest: Chandler, Jeff, Payton, David, and Taylor. From oldest to youngest: Payton, Taylor, Chandler, Jeff, and David.

67. SUBTRACTING UP

Use Roman numerals. If you take away I from XIV, you're left with XV.

68. WORD SOUP

TOUCHDOWN, ALBATROSS, NOSTALGIC, MOTORBOAT, SNAKEBITE, EGREGIOUS, FIDUCIARY, AFFIDAVIT, GALVANIZE

69. MATHEMATICAL MADNESS

3	–	2	x	5	=	5
+		x		x		
4	+	8	+	7	=	19
x		–		+		
9	–	1	x	6	=	48
=		=		=		
63		15		41		

70. WHAT'S A LITTLE DEATH AMONG FRIENDS?

The poison was in the ice cubes. Jack didn't ingest much of it because he drank his gin quickly, and the ice cubes didn't melt. But Jay lingered over his gin and the ice cubes melted, so he got a full dose of poison.

71. IDIOMATIC IDIOSYNCRASIES

The missing letter is W. The idiom is "Kill two birds with one stone."

72. INTO THE WILD

At 39 cents an ounce, a pound comes to $6.24.
Sunflower seeds: 10 ounces ($3.60)
Raisins: 3 ounces ($1.29)
Nuts: 3 ounces ($1.35)

73. SEQUENTIAL THINKING

F and S—the first letters from the words in this series:
Two, Four, Six, Eight, Ten, Twelve, Fourteen, Sixteen.

74. MIRROR, MIRROR

ROTATOR, CIVIC, LEVEL

75. THE GREAT ESCAPE

Inspector Loo waited for nightfall and then went out the second window.

76. PHONE IT IN

1. Clooney
2. Shatner
3. Winfrey

77. INSPECTOR LOO AND THE CASE OF THE BURGER JOINT BURGLARY

Inspector Loo had the other officers arrest Tank. His story didn't make sense. If the red-shirted and blue-shirted guys were an agent and an embezzler (in whatever order), they wouldn't have said what they did. Their statements contradict each other and create a logical paradox. So Tank must have lied when relaying the story, meaning Tank is the embezzler and the culprit.

78. FRATERNAL TRIPLETS

lights, tights, eights

79. WILD & WOOLLY WORDY

Line up in alphabetical order

80. ECHOES
Fined (for a) find

81. BACKWORDS
JOKER, GYPSY

82. YOU'RE GETTING WARMER
Here's one way to do it: SNOW, SLOW, SLOT, SLIT, SLID, SAID, RAID, RAIN

83. A PERFECT GUEST
Yes

84. LETTER MASH
TURKEY, KIMONO, HOORAY, AMBUSH, MERLOT, RIVALS

85. TOP THIS
$16. Each topping is priced by where its first letter comes in the alphabet. P is the 16th letter.

86. LANDSCAPER LAND

Sodder: Zack

Planter: Carlos

Supervisor: Abbott

Waterer: Vernon

Seeder: Buzz

Hole digger: Mark

Reel mower: Tony

Power mower: Hank

Rider mower: Dan

87. LANGUAGE EQUATION

18 Holes on a Golf Course

88. WORD MYSTERY Brother

89. QUICK TRICK JEEP, SEDAN, COUPE

90. RIDDLER

The answer is coal, which starts out black but becomes a diamond in the rough after Mother Earth "smothers" it for a few million years.

91. MOTHER KNOWS BEST?

He took out a classified ad in the newspaper and included all 25 words. (Or he wrote a letter to the editor that included all the words.)

92. ADD 'EM UP

432 + 432 = 864

93. WORD SWAP

1. Treat/Rage

2. Shave/Mane

3. Swoop/Tan

94. TRICK QUESTION

1. No

2. Yes

3. Obviously, this question can't be answered, but you can still get three correct answers if you address the question in the intro: "Can you get more than two of these questions right?"

95. PILFERER OF PERSIA

Daser stole Aribis's gold glazing powder.

96. TOOTHPICK ADDITION

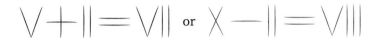

97. SOLAR HIGH-JINKS

Oahu is no different from any other place. At sunset, the sun is 1,000 miles farther away from any point on Earth than it is at noon.

98. INSIDE THE ACTORS' CLASSROOM

The three correct answers don't all have to be different actors: the correct first answer is Cary Grant, the second is John Wayne, and the third is Cary Grant again.

99. WILD & WOOLLY WORDY

Forgives and forgets (four "gives" and four "gets")

100. SUM FUN!

3 + 1 + 8 + 4 + 5 + 9 + 7 = 37

101. AND THE NUMBER IS...?

The bottle weighs 6 ounces; the water weighs 12 ounces.

102. READ BETWEEN THE LINES

1. Threadbare, **2.** Preadolescent, **3.** Retread

103. BACKTRACKING

1. POOR, PORT, HOOT, SPOT, SOOT, SORT

2. EAVE, TARO, TAPE, ROPE, RAVE, PAVE

104. BONUS PAY

Englebert's logic went like this: "If I don't have grease on my nose, then Ben and Flaherty saw the grease on each other's noses but didn't see any on mine. If that had been the case, one of them would have said so. Since neither of them did, I must have grease on my nose, too."

105. WILD & WOOLLY WORDY

Long johns

106. FRATERNAL TRIPLETS

regress, repress, redress

107. RAPID FIRE

• They're two in a set of triplets.

• AGE: the rest are anagrams of other words: TOP, WON, and TEA.

108. A CLOWN-UNDRUM

He juggled the gold bricks as he crossed. That way, one was in the air at all times, and only two bricks (plus Plungy himself) put weight on the bridge.

109. LANGUAGE EQUATION

Nine Innings in a Baseball Game

110. SAM LOYD CLASSIC: THE CASHIER'S PROBLEM

You'd have to give him five $1 bills, fifty $2 bills, and nineteen $5 bills.

111. IT'S SYMBOLIC

Use a decimal point: 4.6

112. THE PROVERB CODE

1. Do as I say, not as I do.

2. A rolling stone gathers no moss.

113. AT THE FAIR

First: Charlie, goats
Second: Annie, llamas

Third: Dustin, pigs
Fourth: Amanda, rabbits

114. BACKTRACKING
1. CAMP, CARP, TAMP, TARP
2. SURE, SOLE, SOUR, SORE, SLUR, LURE

115. NESTED WORDS
IRK in QUIRKS

116. MATH TRICK
124,578. You'll get it every time.

117. THE VACATIONERS
Matt arrived on Sunday and wore the blue baseball cap. Theo arrived on Monday and wore the black sun visor. Mike arrived on Tuesday and wore brown flip-flops. Winston arrived on Wednesday and wore camo capris.

118. WILD & WOOLLY WORDY
Fat chance

119. MONEY TALKS
Green peppers cost $14, carrots were $6, and cucumbers were $5...for a total of $25.

120. MISSING NUMBERS
1637 + 5842 = 7479

121. CURIOUS CONNECTIONS
CHIMPS is the word that belongs. The letters of each word are in alphabetical order.

122. HE SHOULDA KNOWN BETTER
August had been married twice to women named Marilyn; he's visited New Orleans once with each of them. Marilyn has been married only once, to August.

123. BACKWORDS DOWEL, KHAKI

124. PARTY GAME
The question should be "How many legs do you have?" A salmon has none, an ostrich two, a lion four, a cricket six, and a jumping spider eight.

125. TEASER

Drop it from a height of 10 feet. That way, it'll fall the first five feet without breaking.

126. OINK, OINK

127. WORDPLAY

polish, Polish

128. FRATERNAL TRIPLETS

wailed, waited, waived

129. ABOVE OR BELOW?

6 goes above the line—when spelled out in English, those numbers have three letters. The numbers below the line have five letters.

130. A TRICKY GIFT

The gold can be cut into five pieces, with weights of 1, 2, 4, 8, and 15 ounces. On the first day, Dad gave Ashley the 1-ounce piece. On the second day, he traded her for the 2-ounce piece. On the third day, he gave her back the 1-ounce piece. On the fourth day, he traded her for the 4-ounce piece, and so on.

131. WATCH YOUR STEP SHOE, SHOT, SOOT, BOOT

132. IDIOMATIC IDIOSYNCRASIES

The missing letter is T. The idiom is "The oldest trick in the book."

133. THINK ABOUT IT

Bring the extra-strength sunscreen because you'd have to be on Mercury. The planet rotates slowly but travels around the Sun very fast. So one year (the time it takes for the planet to travel around the Sun) takes about 88 Earth days. But one day (the time from sunrise to sunrise) takes 176 Earth days.

134. QUOTE ME "kissing a pretty girl" / "kiss"

135. MIRROR, MIRROR
SOLOS (or ROTOR), REFER, REDDER

136. BACK TO SCHOOL
Monday: Dad, math class
Tuesday: Mom, science class
Wednesday: Aunt Sue, English class

137. LANGUAGE EQUATION
One Giant Leap for Mankind

138. POCKET CHANGE
You've got $1.19 in change: one 50-cent piece, one quarter, four dimes, and four pennies.

139. WILD & WOOLLY WORDY
A raise in pay

140. WHAT ARE THE ODDS?
Both are equally likely. If you and your partner are dealt all the cards in a single suit, that means your competitors have none of that suit. Because the two situations have to happen together, they're equally probable.

141. CLASSROOM ANTICS

Since their statements contradict each other and the boy from the large classroom has to be lying, the student from the small classroom is telling the truth, which makes him a boy, too, meaning Sam is telling the truth.

142. P-P-P-POKER CHIPS

1. Move the chip in the bottom right corner and put it on top of the middle one in the top row.

2. Move the first chip in the bottom row and put it on top of the one that's on the far left in the top row.

3. Move the far right chip in the top row and put it on top of the middle chip in the center column.

143. TELLING TIME

5:00 p.m.

144. THIS OR THAT

Yard

145. BACKWORDS

EXCEL, SHRED

146. ANAGRAM THIS
SUFFOCATED, INDISCREET, MICROSCOPE

147. RAPID FIRE
• MISCHANCE or MECHANICS
• The letter Q

148. A SWELL SUMMER VACATION
Mrs. Moneybags departed at 2:05 for Rome via airplane, Junior Moneybags left at 2:19 for Paris by boat, and Mr. Moneybags departed at 3:32 for London on a train.

149. ECHOES
Paws pause

150. IT ALL ADDS UP
A $50, a $5, and four $2 bills.

151. WEEKLY WONDERINGS
Yesterday, today, and tomorrow

152. PHONE IT IN

1. Presley

2. Kennedy

3. Clinton

153. INSPECTOR LOO AND THE FINE ART OF DETECTION

SCREEN MICE = CRIME SCENE

COIF REFS = OFFICERS

FERN STRIPING = FINGERPRINTS

PROFIT SNOT = FOOTPRINTS

CABLE RIM = CRIME LAB

CREVICED TEENA = TRACE EVIDENCE

PET ART CLASS = PLASTER CAST

AIRY HARPS = HAIR SPRAY

COOL POINTERS = INSPECTOR LOO

154. MIXED MESSAGE

We found three: REALIST, RETAILS, and SALTIER.

155. SEQUENTIAL THINKING

365. The number 42,365 repeats in groups of three.

156. LANGUAGE EQUATION

100 Senators in Congress

157. NESTED WORDS

ape in paper

158. SUM FUN!

A = 1, B = 9, C = 8. The equation is as follows:

```
   1,111
   9,999
 +8,888
 _____
  19,998
```

159. AND THE AGES ARE...

Their ages are 9, 2, and 2. There are only two possible trios of numbers that work here: 1/6/6 and 2/2/9. Since there's an "eldest" daughter, the answer has to be the second choice.

160. ALL OR SOME?

b. No Biggles are Giggles

161. BACKWORDS
IGLOO, YACHT

162. SEQUENTIAL THINKING
Illinois. The states are arranged in the order that they appear on a Monopoly board, starting at Go and working clockwise.

163. ANALOGY LESSON
c. RAT STAR. All four are palindromes.

164. THE ALL-NEW ADVENTURES OF SUPERMOM
Poe, Hallie, Sam, Moe, Joe, Sally, Ali, Callie, Tally, Pete

165. STARRY, STARRY PUZZLE 20

166. SWEET TOOTH
Joan has three jelly beans, one of each color.

167. QUICK TRICK
$101 - 10^2 = 1$

168. WILD & WOOLLY WORDY

A little behind in my work

169. ECHOES

Gene's jeans

170. THE SPACE COWBOYS

Duke, the beer drinker, was from the *Endeavor*; he won $3,000.

Bronco Billy, the bourbon drinker, was from the *Galileo*; he won $2,000.

Frank, the scotch drinker, was from the *Pegasus*; he won $1,000.

Tumbleweed Ted, the whiskey drinker, was from the *Intrepid*; he lost $2,000.

Jesse, the gin drinker, was from the *Traveler*; he lost $4,000.

171. A BERRY GOOD PUZZLE

38. (He took 40 total.)

172. A CLASSIC

The one that doesn't work; it's right twice a day.

173. WHAT'S MISSING?

4. Add the first and third numbers, and then multiply the second and fourth numbers. The answers will be the same.

174. RIDDLER

The word "ton."

175. FRATERNAL TRIPLETS

fleshed, flushed, flashed

176. WORD MYSTERY

Captain

177. MAKING THE SCENE

Hot dogs and mint cookies

178. ELEPHANT RIDE

55 feet total: the elephant rose 10 feet four times, and it dropped 5 feet three times.

179. COUNT 'EM 20

180. HIDDEN WORDS

DISC, DISCO, IS, SCONCE, CON, CONCERT, ON, ONCE, TIN, IN

181. SPLIT CITIES

Albany, Austin, Boston, Denver, Helena, Pierre, Topeka. "NTO" isn't used.

182. LANGUAGE EQUATION

Four Quarters in a Football Game

183. A COLORFUL OUTING

Arlo: red paint, red fatigues
Howard: yellow paint, brown fatigues
Allan: blue paint, yellow fatigues
Rhonda: brown paint, blue fatigues

184. THROW AWAY THE KEY!

Here's one way to do it: TALE, TALL, TAIL, JAIL

185. ANAGRAMMIT

MASTERMIND, QUOTATIONS, MELANCHOLY

186. EXTREME MAKEOVER: LOGIC PUZZLE EDITION

The team of one kid and two dads will win.

187. LIAR, LIAR, PANTS ON FIRE!

The third student was lying. The second boy's statement must have been true because if it were false, both he and the first boy would be wrongdoers.

188. THE CLEVER SERVANTS

Brian, 18 years; Robert, 24 years; and Jiggs, 32 years.

189. SQUARE PEGS

Clockwise from the north hole: A is red, C is yellow, B is green, and D is blue.

190. CHAIN REACTION

BOUNTY hunter GREEN
FINAL four SQUARE

191. TREED

1. Yourself

2. Great-grandfather

3. Great-aunt

192. BACKTRACKING

1. SNOB, SOIL, SOLE, SILL, SEER, LEER

2. ÉLAN, ELSE, EASE, LANE, LOSE, LOSS, BANS, BANE, BASE, BASS, BOSS, NOSE

193. SAM LOYD CLASSIC: A TRICKY PROBLEM

$11 + 1 + 1 + 1 = 14$ (Or any of its variations.)

194. GUESS WHO'S NOT COMING TO DINNER?

No. His wife died many years ago of a heart attack. He's got a portrait of her in the living room. (Another possibility is that her ashes are in an urn on the mantle.)

195. MOON OVER IT

Yes. Since February has only 28 days, you could see a full moon at the beginning and end of January, no full moon in February, and then two more at the beginning and end of March. (The exception would be a leap year, when February has 29 days. It would still be possible to get two moons in January or March, but in that case, you couldn't skip February.)

196. DELI DELIGHTS
$9. Vowels are worth $6, consonants are $3.

197. WHAT'S NEXT?
3079. Each number is increased by 369.

198. SHOPPING SPREE
There were 14 pages in the magazine. Lisa tore out pages 7 and 8.

199. THE FORGETFUL RACING FAN
Caveman

200. WORDPLAY
If you remove the first letter from each word, you end up with another word: (s)cent, (g)nu, (h)our, (k)not, (a)isle, (w)hole.

201. CONNECTIONS
You can add the letters -ant to the end of each word to get a new word: ADAMANT, BUOYANT, CLAIMANT, GALLANT, and RAMPANT.

202. WILD & WOOLLY WORDY Last but not least

203. SEQUENTIAL THINKING
17. The numbers correspond to the letters' place in the alphabet, but we've only included consonants. B is second, C is third, and so on. Q is 17th.

204. THE MAGIC SQUARE
1. Each half row or column adds up to 130.

2. Each 2 x 2 square also adds up to 130.

3. The four corner boxes add up to 130.

4. The four corners and the four center boxes all add up to 260.

5. The four boxes that run diagonally from the corners plus their mates on the other side (e.g., 52–54 and 43–45) equal 260.

6. The four two-box diagonals in each corner add up to 260.

7. The eight corners of any two 4 x 4 squares add up to 260.

205. HEY, SPORTS FANS
Baseball

206. LANGUAGE EQUATION
Five Digits in a ZIP Code

207. KNOW WHEN TO HOLD 'EM
From left to right: three of diamonds, Jack of diamonds, Jack of hearts.

208. GRANDMOTHER TIME
Grandma Agnes was 72.

209. ECHOES
Mean mien

210. WORD MYSTERY Blanket

211. THINK ON IT
Uncle John found civvies, divvy, flivver, revved, and savvy...and any of their variations. (If you also came up

with "navvy"—which means "unskilled laborer"—we salute your spectacular vocabulary!)

212. NUMBER FUN

1	4	7
3	6	2
5	8	9

213. WATCH OUT!

Peter was sitting in a tree. Lightning hit and killed him.

214. BONES OF CONTENTION

The youngest dog is 7 (he started with 4 bones), the middle one is 10 (he started with 7), and the oldest is 16 (he started with 13).

215. A TRIP DOWN LIAR'S LANE

Both men are lying. If John's statements are true, Scott is a Smith from the top of the hill. If John's statements are false, Scott is a Jones from the bottom of the hill. Either way, Scott is a liar. Therefore, Scott's statements have to be false, which makes John a Smith from the top of the hill. But because Smiths who live at the top of the hill lie, John's statements are also false, making Scott a Jones from the bottom of the hill.

216. TRICKY MATH

4 fingers + 1 thumb = 1 hand

217. THE DISASTROUS DERBY

The four winning horses that day were Break a Leg, Chokes Before Finish, Lags Behind, and Sir Cries a Lot. Since the friends picked only one winner apiece, Break a Leg had to have won one of the races (clue #4).

Since Bud was the only one to bet on Chokes Before Finish, Brad was the only one to bet on Lags Behind, and Byron was the only one to bet on Sir Cries a Lot, those must have been the winners of the other three races.

218. MOMMY AND ME

Pink stroller: Bootsy, wearing soft shoes, mom is Laura

Purple stroller: Michael, wearing a T-shirt, mom is Joanne

Green stroller: Bo, wearing a bib, mom is Bonnie

Blue stroller: Caitlin, wearing a onesie, mom is Susan

Yellow stroller: Pebbles, wearing a baseball cap, mom is Jane

219. BACKWORDS

COVER, QUOTA

220. DYNAMIC TRIOS

Famous couples: **1.** Antony & Cleopatra, **2.** Barbie & Ken, **3.** Brad Pitt & Angelina Jolie

221. GENDER ROLES

-er. It changes "widow" to "widower."

222. SEQUENTIAL THINKING

2520. Multiply each number sequentially by 3, 4, 5, 6, and 7.

223. ECHOES   Cruise crews

224. MONEY TALKS

Say "I won't take the $1 bill or the $5 bill." If you're telling the truth, you'll get the $10 bill. If your statement is a lie, the reverse must be true and you would take the $1 or the $5 bill. However, that violates the terms of the setup (that you get no money if you don't tell the truth). So you must be telling the truth with your first statement.

225. WILD & WOOLLY WORDY

Take from the rich and give to the poor

226. YIKES!

Andy will wait for the merry-go-round ride to end...and then he'll dismount.

227. FRATERNAL TRIPLETS poet, pout, post

228. THREES PLEASE
1. $3 + 3 + 3 \times 3 - 3 = 24$
2. $3 - 3 + 3 - 3 \times 3 = 0$
3. $3 \times 3 - 3 \times 3 \div 3 = 6$

229. INSPECTOR LOO AND THE INTERRUPTED STROLL

In most states, buses carrying paying passengers are required to stop at railroad crossings. Because the bus sped up to get over the tracks and make the light, Inspector Loo deduced that it was the escape vehicle.

230. COIN TOSS
1 in 2, for every single toss

231. CLASSIC Skin on a cow

232. UP AND DOWN

There were 19 rungs. She started in the middle, went up six, down eight, up three, and up eight, for a total of nine rungs above where she began: 9 above + 9 below + the middle rung = 19.

233. DIGITAL ARCHITECTURE

123 is the magic number.

$1 + 2 + 3 = 6$

$1 \times 2 \times 3 = 6$

$6 - 6 = 0$

234. PREFERENCES

He prefers 64. Uncle John likes numbers that are perfect squares.

235. MATH CIPHER

1462	−	297	=	1165
÷		−		−
43	+	272	=	315
34	x	25	=	850

236. LET'S PLAY CARDS

SOLITAIRE, GIN, BRIDGE, SPADES, HEARTS

237. WORD FIND   Aggravate

238. WILD & WOOLLY WORDY   Mixed-doubles tennis

239. I'LL BET YA

One-eff Jef ran around the chair twice and then said, "I'll be back in a week to run around a third time," knowing that Two-eff Jeff would have to get up by then.

240. A NUMBERS GAME

9	10	9
8	7	8
10	7	10

241. "HONE" IN ON IT

1. Dishonest, **2.** Megaphone, **3.** Phonetics

242. IDIOMATIC IDIOSYNCRASIES

The missing letter is A. The idiom is "dead as a doornail."

243. THE FAIRY FASHION SHOW

The Blue Fairy got to the show at 3:04 p.m. (4 minutes late) because she'd misplaced her wand; she wore the jeweled crown.

The Green Fairy arrived at 3:10 p.m. (10 minutes late) because she'd spilled fairy dust all over her living room; she wore the magic shoes.

The Yellow Fairy got to the show at 3:12 p.m. (12 minutes late) because her ladybug roommates had hidden her wings; she wore the feathered dress.

244. PASS THE BASKET

Bob keeps chickens. He put his rooster in the basket and gave it to his friend.

245. LANGUAGE EQUATION

Two Houses of Congress

246. THINK ABOUT IT

An hourglass—it has thousands of grains of sand.

247. THE PROVERB CODE

1. Easy come, easy go.

2. Don't count your chickens before they hatch.

248. SEQUENTIAL THINKING

39. Use subtraction: 74 − 9, 65 − 8, 57 − 7, etc.

249. THIS OR THAT Carp

250. THREE'S THE KEY 33 3/3

251. ECHOES Foul fowl

252. SHOP 'TIL YOU DROP

45. The iron cost $22, the radio $10, the buttons $4, and the candy $1.

253. FLIP-FLOPPED

1. Mishmash, **2.** Knickknack, **3.** Fiddle-faddle

254. TO BE OR NOT TO B

There's nothing wrong with them. They're all real words...either variants (like "employe"), or they have their own definitions (like "skat."). All four appear in *Merriam-Webster's Collegiate Dictionary, 11th Edition.*

255. DOUBLE TROUBLE

The couples are Jennifer and Ben (liar) Murphy, Kelly and Dan (liar) Webb, and Allen and Britney (liar) Carroll.

256. WORD MASH   Quibbler

257. AROUND THE WORLD   Tokyo and Kyoto, Japan

258. WEDDING PARTY

Lauren's husband was Zac, who brought lilies. Allison's husband was James, who brought roses. Morgan's husband was Brian, who brought sunflowers.

258

259. TEASER
The Pirates are an all-female team.

260. WILD & WOOLLY WORDY
But on second thought...

261. NAME GAME
We came up with one: John. The female names are Joan, Jen, June, Jan, Jane, and Jean.

262. A PARTY FOR THE AGES
Audrey was 16, Danny was 12, Vicki was 10, the triplets (Daisy, Gabi, and Max) were 8, and Josie was 4.

263. RIDDLER
Corps

264. WILD RIDE
1. Rob, whose survival skill was climbing trees and whose luxury item was a book of brainteasers.

2. Jen, whose survival skill was making fire and whose luxury item was lipstick.

3. Jake, whose survival skill was swimming and whose luxury item was shampoo.

4. Lucy, whose survival skill was gathering fruit and whose luxury item was shaving cream.

265. IN YOUR ESTIMATION...

There are about 12.5 penny thicknessness in a penny's diameter.

266. THE CASE OF THE MISSING LETTERS

1. Teammate, **2.** Legible

267. WORD MATH

26. The words are assigned values based on the position of their first letter in the alphabet. F (for FRONT) is 6th and B (for BACK) is 2nd, for a total of 8. M appears 13th in the alphabet, and 13 + 13 = 26.

268. GROWING DOWN

Here's one way to do it: MAN, BAN, BAY, BOY

269. THE NAME'S THE GAME

Dan was Ben's brother, and he drove a dune buggy named Michael. The others: Brad drove a pickup truck named Dan. Michael, a motorcycle named Ben. Aaron, a Porsche named Brad. Ben, a VW van named Aaron.

270. A CIRCUITOUS ROUTE

Sacred, clever, cowboy, icebox, quirks, violet

271. INSPECTOR LOO INVESTIGATES A MURDER ON THE HIGH SEAS

Inspector Loo noticed that Reagan's gun holster was on his left hip, implying that he was left-handed. Yet, in his left hand, Reagan was holding the office keys; the gun was positioned in his right hand. That meant Reagan couldn't have been holding the gun when he was shot.

As soon as Loo presented this evidence, Joe Thornton confessed. He'd been riffling through the captain's things looking for the cash box when Reagan caught him in the act. Thornton shot Reagan and staged the scene to look like a break-in. Thornton was hauled off to the brig, where he spent the remainder of the trip. The porter (after a stern talking-to by the captain) kept his job.

272. WHAT'S UP, TEACH?

Ten minutes. Monty said that if his wife hadn't sent the text, he'd have driven twice as long, losing one hour. That means that if he'd gone home and then had to return to school to get the homework, it would have taken him two hours (or 120 minutes).

That drive would have consisted of three legs (school to home, home to school, and school to home) to go back and retrieve the homework, so each leg is 40 minutes long.

Since Monty said the text saved him an hour, it would have taken him 30 minutes to get home from where he was in his drive and another 30 minutes to get back to that spot. That means he was 30 minutes from home when he got his wife's text, or 10 minutes (40 total minus 30 left) into his commute.

273. RIDDLER Silence

274. QUICK TRICK 52 – 3 x 4 = 196

275. SAM LOYD CLASSIC: RIDING AGAINST THE WIND

The most common answer is this: If a rider goes a mile in

3 minutes with the wind, and returns against the wind in 4 minutes, so 3 and 4 equals 7 and should give a correct average, so that his time would be $3\frac{1}{2}$ minutes. But that's incorrect because the wind helped him for only 3 minutes, and it worked against him for 4 minutes.

So if he can ride a mile in 3 minutes with the wind, he could go $1\frac{1}{3}$ mile in 4 minutes, and one mile in 4 minutes against the wind. Therefore $2\frac{1}{3}$ miles in 8 minutes gives his actual speed because the wind helped him as much as it hindered him. So the rider's actual speed for a single mile without any wind would be 3 minutes and $25\frac{5}{7}$ seconds.

276. SCIENCE SUPERSTARS

First place: Alison, who built the talking robot

Second place: Max, who grew mold

Third place: Brendan, who made a comet

Fourth place: Melissa, who studied whether or not classical music helped plants grow

277. ANAGRAMMIT

HESITATION, ADVENTURES, RESTAURANT

278. FRATERNAL TRIPLETS

maze, daze, gaze

279. A LEAF FROM THE FAMILY TREE

Lea is Janet's grandmother.

280. THE BOSS'S BIG IDEA

Each pilot was flying the other's plane.

281. REUNITED

Seating order from left to right: Jamie Walsh, Trisha Romanov, Katie Grant, Jack Garcia, Dana Jones, and Eddie Smith

282. WILD & WOOLLY WORDY   Square meals

283. MORE THAN ONE WAY TO SKIN A CAT

Out of sight, out of mind.

284. PREFERENCES

Aunt Abby likes things that begin with consecutive letters: *Op*als, *De*ans, *No*bles, and *Hi*biscuses. (Just like her name: *Ab*by.)

285. IT'S ALL ELEMENTAL

Boron, oxygen, neon, iron, argon, tin, barium, zinc

286. BIRTHDAY BONUS

Alex's birthday is on December 31. Today is January 1. The day before yesterday was December 30 of last year. On Alex's most recent birthday (yesterday), he turned 18. The day before yesterday (December 30), he was 17. Today is a new year. So on this year's December 31, he'll turn 19. And next year, he'll turn 20.

287. TEASER

The coffee was sweet. Luke had put sugar in it before he noticed the piece of plastic.

288. BACKWORDS

OUGHT, SKIRT

289. FRATERNAL TRIPLETS

starting, starling, starving

290. A NUMBERS GAME

$$
\begin{array}{r}
225 \\
\times\ 225 \\
\hline
50,625
\end{array}
$$

291. INSPECTOR LOO AND THE CRYPTO CLUB

To get in, you had to answer with a word that started with the first letter of the first word in Soup's question—Who/Wordsworth, How/Hercules, etc.

292. WILD & WOOLLY WORDY

Foreign language ("for" in "language")

293. WORD MASH Aardvark

294. QUICK TRICK

$12 + 3 \times 4 - 5 \times 6 - 78 \div 9 = 28$

295. TRUTH OR LIE?

It's Tuesday—Anya is telling the truth.

296. THIS WAS NO PICNIC

The three men drank eight bottles of water, or 2⅔ each. Subtracting 2⅔ from the five bottles the first traveler brought means he gave the third man 2⅓ bottles. Subtracting 2⅔ from the three bottles of the second traveler means he gave ⅓ of a bottle. So the ratio for dividing up the money is 2⅓ to ⅓—or 7 to 1; the first man should get seven of the eight coins, and the second man should get one.

297. MATHEMATICAL MADNESS

1	+	4	x	8	=	40
+		x		x		
6	+	9	+	3	=	18
x		-		+		
5	-	2	x	7	=	21
=		=		=		
35		34		31		

298. RAPID FIRE

- The word "wholesome"
- She was walking at the time.

299. SEQUENTIAL THINKING

22. If you spell out all of the numbers in English, they each contain the letter "O." Twenty-two is the next one.

300. QUOTE ME "Immortality"

301. SUNDAY DRIVE

Bernie Welloff was driving the Porsche. His passenger was Jack.

302. NO PARK-ING

The friends will meet up on February 21.

303. BICYCLE BOON OR BUST?

She made $20. Think of it as two transactions: She first bought the bike for $40 and sold it for $50. Then she bought it for $60 and sold it for $70. She made $10 each time.

304. INSPECTOR LOO AND THE CASE OF THE SILK STOCKINGS

The first suspect must have told the shopkeeper that he owned a white coat. (Otherwise, Loo could not have identified the other suspects.) If that statement were true, both of the statements of the other two men would be false, so the first man must be lying. Since he's lying but doesn't own a white coat, he must own the blue one and must be the thief.

305. TRICKY, TRICKY

White. The license plate stands for "I'm late, I'm late," the signature saying of the White Rabbit in the 1951 Disney film *Alice in Wonderland*. Because the car was a Volkswagen hatchback with that particular license plate, the model must've been a Rabbit. Thus, the car was white, i.e., a "white Rabbit."

306. CELESTIAL WORDPLAY

Here's one way to do it: STAR, SOAR, BOAR, BOOR, BOON, MOON

307. LOOKING FOR LINCOLN

No. Abraham Lincoln appears on both sides of the $5 bill. The front image is obvious, but the bill's back image is of the Lincoln Memorial, and the president's statue is tiny, but visible.

308. BACKTRACKING

1. SEER, SITE, SIRE, STIR, STET, TIME, TIER, TIRE, MERE

2. LACE, LAIN, LATE, CITE, ITEM, TEAM, YANG

309. CONNECTIONS

They describe Snow White's seven dwarfs: Grumpy, Dopey, Sneezy, Sleepy, Bashful, Doc, and Happy.

310. ECHOES

Flee (a) flea

311. FILL 'ER UP

Fill up the nine-ounce glass and then use that glass to fill up the other one. You'll have five ounces left in the first glass. Empty the four-ounce glass and do it again. Now you have one ounce left in the nine-ounce glass.

Empty the four-ounce glass and put that last one ounce into it. Keep it there. Fill up the nine-ounce glass again, and then use it to fill the remaining space in the four-ounce glass. That will take away three ounces, and you'll be left with six ounces in the nine-ounce glass.

312. IDIOMATIC IDIOSYNCRASIES

The missing letter is T. The idiom is "The early bird catches the worm."

313. A NUMBERS GAME

$$
\begin{array}{r}
52 \\
\times\ 52 \\
\hline
104 \\
260 \\
\hline
2704 \\
\end{array}
$$

314. TRICKY, TRICKY

In the first row, the numbers (when spelled out) all have four letters; in the second row, they all have three; and in the third row they all have two. In addition, the words appear in alphabetical order in each row.

315. THE CASE OF THE MISSING LETTERS

1. Stardust, **2.** Andean

316. THE PROVERB CODE

1. A man who is his own lawyer has a fool for a client.
2. A woman's work is never done.

317. THE CANTERBURY COOK-OFF

Cakes

1. Anna (age 20)
2. Jonathan (age 23)
3. Lisa (age 24)
4. Sean (age 21)

Cookies

1. Sean
2. Jonathan
3. Anna
4. Lisa

318. AROUND THE WORD

We found 22 words: BEG, EGG, GOAT, OAT, GOATEE,

ATE, TEE, EEL, ELM, MAP, APE, APEX, EXIT, ITEM, TEMP, PEW, EWE, WED, WEDGE, EDGE, GURU, REB.

319. BACKWORDS REVEL, EARTH

320. TREED
1. Grandmother
2. Stepmother

321. CAN YOU UNMAKE THIS MESS?
The kids picked up 102 toys. Joey picked up 18 dolls and 16 blocks, Emma picked up 6 dolls and 28 blocks, and Bryce picked up 27 dolls and 7 blocks.

322. RIDDLER A golf ball

323. DIRTY DOGS
First: Sparkles, Frisbee catch.
Second: Bubba, juggled water bowls.
Third: Meathead, herded mechanical squirrels

324. A NUMBERS GAME

```
    25
  x 25
  ─────
   125
    50
  ─────
   625
```

325. PREFERENCES

The kangaroo. Olivia prefers things whose names include the letter "o."

326. SAY "UNCLE!"

1st: Abe

2nd: Hank

3rd: Chris

4th: Cisco

327. RAPID FIRE

• A volcano

• 9 + 9 + 99 + 99 + 999 = 1,215 (or any variation thereof)

328. DYNAMIC TRIOS

Famous friends: **1.** Bert & Ernie, **2.** Laverne & Shirley,
3. Matt Damon & Ben Affleck

329. THE INHERITANCE

Linda got $10,000.

Arlen got $20,000.

Jackie got $40,000.

Stan got $80,000.

330. BACKWORDS ONION, WITCH

331. A PUZZLING TRIP Everyone on board was married.

332. LETTER PLAY

1. Letters on the bottom row of a computer keyboard.

2. The three most common blood types.

333. TRICKY, TRICKY

There's no letter "e" anywhere in the paragraph.

334. PUT ME IN, COACH!

Vinnie Jr. (Matt Jr. played shortstop, and Ronnie Jr. pitched.)

335. CONNECTIONS

The letters in each word can be rearranged to spell different animals: horse, goat, manatee, parrot, and sardine.

336. WHAT'S HIS LINE OF WORK?

Max: pool hustler and street musician
Bert: bricklayer and bartender
Cameron: gambler and physician

337. LANGUAGE EQUATION

Ten Dimes in a Dollar

338. WORD SCRAMBLE

The subject is "DOGS." The related words are different breeds: BLOODHOUND, BOXER, BULLDOG, COLLIE, POODLE.

339. WORD MYSTERY
Trombone

340. KOUNTING KIDS
Mrs. Kantor is 28; the younger child is 5, and the twins are 8. The three-digit number is 588.

341. INSPECTOR LOO AND THE CASE OF THE MURDERED MATRON
Andrew McCann said he turned on the air conditioner when he got home, *after* he found his wife's body. But the buttercream cupcake frosting was stiff. Had it really been left in the sweltering heat all afternoon, with Tamara dead on the floor, it would have melted. Thus, Andrew McCann was lying.

342. CURIOUS CONNECTIONS
Each of the words in the top list can morph into a musical instrument by changing one letter: CUBA to TUBA, DRAM to DRUM, CRUMPET to TRUMPET, and then HARP, FIDDLE, and CELLO. The word in the bottom list that belongs is FINE, which can change to FIFE.

343. ANAGRAMMIT

CAPITALIST, GOVERNMENT, BAMBOOZLED

344. A FUNNY SITUATION

Zeno has 28 students: 14 + 7 + 4 + 3 = 28.

345. SAM LOYD CLASSIC: PUZZLING PRATTLE

Sunday

346. WORDPLAY

The word is CATCHPHRASE.

347. CASTLE RESTAURANTS Yes

348. PIE CUTS

There were two ways for Christine to do this: **1.** Her first cut was circular, around the center of the pie. Her next two cuts crossed the pie's center at right angles. Or **2.** Her first two cuts were overlapping arcs, and her third cut went down the center of the pie.

349. AGE HAZE

Mrs. Barnes is 36, Mary Jane is 12, and Larissa and Ben are both 8.

350. FOUR SQUARE

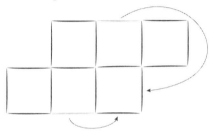

351. QUICK TRICK

David's dad was 39 when David was 13.

352. CANDY MAGIC

The cheap one cost 20 cents; the fancy one, $3.20.

353. FRATERNAL TRIPLETS

tease, tense, terse

354. LETTER PERFECT
There are eight E's, two O's, and six T's in this sentence.

355. SEQUENTIAL THINKING
97432. Move the numbers to the right one space and put the last number in front each time.

356. WILD & WOOLLY WORDY A drop in temperature

357. POKER PARADOX
Rick gave Jane his $5.10, and she gave him a quarter in change. Then Jane gave $1 to Judd, and he gave her 35¢. Lastly, Jane gave Harriet $5.45 of her $5.95, and Harriet gave Jane $4.05 in change.

358. FIVE-FINGER DISCOUNT
Sarah: doll, first floor
May: power drill, second floor
Ryan: baseball, second floor
James: soaps, third floor
Ann: earrings, fourth floor
Ellen: bedspread, fifth floor

359. VOWEL PLAY Queueing

360. WILD & WOOLLY WORDY Hard up

361. ONE SIDE OR THE OTHER. The river was frozen.

362. FRATERNAL TRIPLETS pride, prime, prize

363. BOOK BITE

The bookworm ate through only $2\frac{1}{2}$" of book. He started on page one of the book on the left (which is facing the right side) and just had to eat through its cover. Then he ate the back cover, interior, and front cover of book two, and the back cover of book three. At that point, he reached the last page of the third book and stopped eating.

364. CHAIN REACTION BLACK board ROOM
BIRD brain STORM

365. MATH TRICK Four

Uncle John's Bathroom Puzzlers: For Puzzle Lovers

Find these and other great Uncle John's Bathroom Reader titles online at ***www.bathroomreader.com***

Or contact us:
Bathroom Readers' Institute
PO Box 1117
Ashland, OR 97520
e-mail: mail@bathroomreader.com

THE LAST PAGE

Fellow Bathroom Readers
The fight for good bathroom puzzling should never be taken loosely—we must do our duty and sit firmly for what we believe in, even while the rest of the world is taking potshots at us.

We'll be brief. Now that we've proven we're not simply a flush-in-the-pan, we invite you to take the plunge: Sit Down and Be Counted! To earn a permanent place on the BRI honor roll, just log on to *www.bathroomreader.com.* No join-up fees, monthly minimums or maximums, organized dance parties, quilting bees, solicitors, annoying phone calls (we only have one phone line), spam—or any other canned meat product—to worry about...just the chance to get our fabulous monthly newsletter and discounts on Bathroom Reader products.

You can also send us a letter:
Bathroom Readers' Institute
PO Box 1117
Ashland, OR 97520

Or email us: mail@bathroomreader.com.

Hope you enjoyed the book. And if you're skipping to the end, go back and finish!